GLASGOW:
DUNN AND WRIGHT,
PRINTERS.

CONTENTS.

THE

CRUSADE OF THE PERIOD.

BY

JOHN MITCHEL.

———

CHAPTER I.

FROUDE *versus* IRELAND.

THE "First of Living Historians," as several newspapers designate this gentleman, is only now really opening his batteries. He has by no means done with his victim, but presses on, with "blow on blow." Even since the termination of the lectures and counter lectures, by the Historian and by Father Burke, there has been published in this country and in England the first volume of a new and elaborate work—"The English in Ireland, in the Eighteenth Century;" by James Anthony Froude, M.A.; a work which sheds additional darkness on a subject which the author has already done much to overwhelm in obscurity. This darkness I shall endeavour presently to dispel in some degree. Meantime the pens not only of national writers in Ireland, but of many fair-minded journalists both in England and the United States are busily employed in making indignant exposures of the spirit and tone of the Historian, as well as of his alleged facts and authorities. The controversy, then, is only beginning.

THE MOCK TRIAL.

This grand plea, lately brought forward so gravely by the Historian, and as gravely tried before the imaginary tribunal of our American public—*this*, indeed, is finished, and got out of the way. Now that all those pleadings are before us, as well as the fresh and formidable indictment set forth in the new book, it may be expedient to review the whole matter. The lectures are carefully reported on either side, and the reports are, doubtless, generally correct; but still (at least so far as Mr Froude's share in them is concerned) they do not seem to have been revised by the author and published as his very words, so that you cannot absolutely hold him to words, figures, dates, and citations of authorities. Here, in this book, we have him with his *litera scripta*, "inverted commas" and all. It may indeed be regretted that the eloquent Father Burke gave any countenance to the Sham Trial; that he innocently accepted the tribunal and pleaded the declaration, in the name of his country; thus materially helping the general plan of the crusade; also that, after bandying compliments with the learned gentleman on the other side, gratuitously affirming and proclaiming that person's honesty, and saying that he loved him, Father Burke ended by giving up the whole case, concurring in his adversary's practical conclusion, turning to his countrymen and telling them plainly that they can do nothing, *nothing*, at home or abroad, to relieve their native island of British domination; and in short that they had better "wait for the *New Zealander !*"

"*Attendez sous l'orme*," is the ironical French proverb to this same effect. "Wait for the New Zealander" will become proverbial in Ireland, in the same derisive sense. When that predestined savage shall be seen squatting upon the broken arch and sketching the ruins of London, *then* Ireland will arise great, glorious and free, first flower, &c. ! Also, when the sky falls, shan't we have larks ?

And so, at the end of the sham "trial," the Historian comes forward with a kind of playful insolence, and seizes on his small triumph with a sneer; congratulates everybody that "for practical objects" he and his opponent are agreed, offers him his hand, and kindly says, "Any how, I hope we part in good humour." Oh! certainly; all the good humour in life, so far as he and Father Burke are concerned; and the sham court rises with a laugh—*solvuntur risu*.

But there are others concerned in this crusading mission of the Historian. And there is, and was, no tribunal at all; it was only the agreeable Englishman's device to flatter this great

American people, by presenting a sort of mimicry of a Geneva
Arbitration to settle international differences by the high and
mighty award of American public opinion. I decline to plead
at all before the American public; because Irishmen are themselves the best and sole judges of the rights and the wrongs of
their own land. Neither can I be a client of the excellent and
eloquent Father Burke in this cause; indeed he excludes me;
for in his second lecture he accepts with thanks and effusion
Froude's statement, that, after the " Reformation," " the cause
of the Catholic religion and Irish independence became inseparably and irrevocably one." As a non-Catholic, then, I am
ruled out of court, as well as Grattan, and Tone, and O'Brien,
and Davis. We are not quite Irish, under this rule. Counsel on
the other side, indeed, is willing to take us under his protection ;
he treats the Irish Protestants as his peculiar and favoured
clients; but I repudiate his advocacy even more earnestly than
the Dominican's. He has obliging things to say concerning
Irish Protestants when they are useful slaves of British policy;
and not being a slave to that policy, I cannot hope to profit by the
author's advocacy. From my own point of view, then, I shall
adventure to survey the whole field on which our Irish cause
lately *appeared* to be debated so earnestly, but from which the
two adversaries have walked off together almost hand-in-hand,
with all the complacency in the world.

The truth is, and it may as well be said, that many of
Father Burke's countrymen have felt disappointed at the soft
and tender usage which he gave, throughout, to that loud and
furious enemy of our native island. Surely, the Dominican
could have struck heavier blows, but that something held
his hand. The two champions, somehow, were unwilling
to hurt each other. Just so, the betting men of sporting
tastes eagerly awaited the battle between Mr Mace and Mr
O'Baldwin. Loud boasts and threats there were, and diplo-
matic correspondence in newspapers, to settle place and prelimi-
naries; men made their books, and thought full surely there
was going to be a real mill : but the two buffers had no idea
of getting hurt, of bruising one another's expressive mugs, or
drawing claret from those aquiline conks : at last they walked
off with their respective backers, and left the betting men in
the lurch.

Yet it is not easy to understand what moved Father Burke to such rather fulsome tenderness of courtesy; for assuredly the First Living Historian prepared the campaign of this foray of his in a manner irritating enough to provoke a saint.

The Historian had written his book, and had sent it to the press, a book full charged with venomous loathing and contempt of the Irish name and nation; and seems to have judged it expedient, for some reason or another, to condense the substance of it into lectures, and to come over and discharge them in American cities, where he supposed he would be sure of a favourable hearing for any abuse of Irish and Catholics amongst the preponderating masses of American Protestants. I suppose he had been told so by some " Christian young men." At any rate the thing would make a stir, and advertise his book. At the very moment when it was convenient for him he was invited by the " Literary Bureau." Whether this was a happy coincidence, or whether he invited the Bureau to invite him, cannot now be guessed; nor is it worth while. His subject was to be " The Relations between England and Ireland;" and his coming was heralded by a pamphlet containing first a fac-simile of his letter of acceptance, and then many pages presenting selected passages from his works, entitled " Gems from Froude." This pamphlet was largely circulated gratuitously. In the letter he considerately says—" I should like it to be understood by the Irish in New York generally that I am neither going to flatter them nor flatter England." Were " the Irish in New York generally " fondly soothing themselves with the idea that Froude was coming to flatter them? Who saw any sign of such pleasing anticipations? In truth, we are not much used to flattery, save from a politician now and then about election times. And those who know very much of the " First Historian's " previous writings could scarcely have looked for anything very fulsome in the way of sycophancy at his hands. Indeed, in these very " Gems," strung together on the thread of this pamphlet, there is but one passage referring to Ireland, which begins thus—

" Sadder history in the compass of the world's great chronicle there is none than the history of the Irish; so courageous, yet so like cowards; so interesting, yet so resolute to forfeit all honourable claims to interest. In thinking of them, we can but shake our heads," &c.

I do not well know how courageous men contrive to be "like cowards;" yet, after all, it seems our people are "interesting;" he never denies this; "interesting," yet "resolute to forfeit honourable claims to interest!" Not only a dishonourable people, but resolutely and irrevocably determined that no honourable person can concern himself about any of them. Differ, we Irish may, on politics, on religion, on many matters of human conduct and life, but at least on one point we are agreed—we are unanimously and irremediably resolved to be *dishonourable!* This is bad, indeed. Let me add to this "gem" another jewel of my own selection from the new volume just published—

"The sun never shone on a lovelier country, as nature made it. *They have pared its forests to the stump,* till it shivers in damp and desolation. The perceptions of taste which belong to the higher orders of understanding are as completely absent as truthfulness of spirit is absent, or cleanliness of person and habit."

No; assuredly the First Living Historian had no mission to flatter the Irish race. But let readers bear in mind the phrase, "They have pared its forests to the stump" until we have advanced a little further with this modest review.

England, the country of the Historian, is in these days disquieted once more by a revival of national spirit and national pretensions in Ireland. "Home Rule" has become a political test. "Irish ideas," even, which England has so often before felt it her duty to stifle in blood—these very Irish ideas are now again put forward as the only just basis on which the island should be governed; and, worse than all, many of the best of the Protestants are cordially uniting with their Catholic fellow-countrymen in demanding some approach to self-government. British policy had often been interfered with by such demonstrations before; and had usually, at least since the "Reformation," found its best safety in promoting religious animosities; the same course must be taken now again; hatred and spite of Protestant against Catholic must be kindled again and fed with fresh fuel, or all is lost. Prudent British statesmen look anxiously around and survey the situation; they see

a considerable Protestant recrudescence in several parts of the
world, provoked ostensibly by the late Council of the Vatican
with its definition of the ancient doctrine of Papal Infallibility.
They see prosperous and triumphant Germany girding up its
loins to do battle with the dreadful Pope ; and Prince Bismarck
is prosecuting bishops and thundering against Jesuits. And
so in the very latest Irish papers I read, without surprise—

"On Monday, criminal informations were filed in the Crown
Office, Dublin, in the names of Mr Christopher Palles and Mr
W. Lane Joynt, against his Lordship the Bishop of Clonfert,
twenty-three Catholic clergymen of the county Galway,
Captain Nolan, and Mr Sebastian Nolan. All these gentlemen
are charged with the use of undue influence, and the Court of
Queen's Bench is asked to 'award due process of law' against
them. The venue is laid in the county Galway, and it appears
that, as the informations are equivalent to bills found by a
Grand Jury on an indictment, the next step will be to put the
Bishop of Clonfert and his fellow-defendants in the dock of the
County Court-house, in Galway, and call on them to plead."

The "undue influence" was in representing to their flocks
that it would be committing a sin to vote for Gladstone's
candidate : and a crying sin it certainly would have been ; and
who could more properly warn them against it than their
clergy ? However, the prosecution itself will excite spite and
rage, unmanly exultation amongst the Orangemen, bitter and
vindictive wrath amongst the Catholics, and thus a great
point is gained to begin with. Next, it is at any time easy
to create exasperation amongst the more ignorant Protestants,
by pointing out the so-called presumption of the Catholic
Church ; and facilities are given to carry on the unholy work
of lashing the two parties to fury by the agitation now existing
on the question of public education. Shall the education of
children be made carefully irreligious? or shall all the people be
required to pay for an irreligious education though they cannot
use the article ? Or shall parents be at liberty, if they choose,
to give to their children a separate denominational education,
without being compelled also to pay for the State education of
other people's children ? Easy enough to alarm the ignorant
persons aforesaid, by a suggestion that this latter plan is nothing
but a device of the Jesuits to bring back the Inquisition. Then,

in turning their eyes anxiously around the horizon, those prudent English statesmen take careful note of the signs of the times in the United States. Here also the State and denominational school systems are eagerly debated. Here also the ignorant masses have been taught to believe that the Infallibility of the Pope, and especially the "Syllabus," are only an insidious machinery for troubling the peace of States and Governments, and making us all vassals to "the Woman who sitteth upon Seven Hills." The English know also (for they have both spies and agents busy here) that, ever since the close of the war, there has been gradually reviving a strong anti-Catholic and anti-Irish feeling which awaits only a good stirring example, set *in England*, to follow suit as usual. An excitement can always be stirred up in America on this principle. It was the "Ecclesiastical Titles Act" to restrain Papal Aggression, that gave birth to our shabby Know-Nothing crusade; and a few bloody riots were duly enacted, a church or two wrecked, a good priest "ridden on a rail," and tarred and feathered by the principal inhabitants of a New England town. A renewal of all this would be invaluable for exasperating the so-desirable religious rage in Ireland.

And there is more in it. Certain millions of the Irish people, extirpated out of their own land, and escaped from the British famines, are now dwelling, they and their children, upon this continent; and everybody knows that they watch with keen interest every national movement of their kindred at home, with the stern determination to bear a hand in the final settlement of that question. Nothing could possibly be more serviceable to Gladstone's policy than the successful arousing of strong dislike and contempt on the part of the Protestant American people against their Catholic and Irish fellow-citizens. Now, no man in all England could be found so fitted for this dreadful office as the First Living Historian.

Froude's qualifications for this mission (besides a most fluent and sensational rhetoric) are twofold. First, he hates the Catholic Church, and has at his fingers' ends all the foulest imputations and all the diabolical language of abuse usually employed these last three hundred years to cover that Church with a robe of blackest horror; second, he claims for his own country an absolute right to possess and govern Ireland at her own will and for her own profit. As I read these pages of the "First Historian," I confess that I warm towards him a little; he does not cant much, for an Englishman, but pours forth his insults upon the people and upon their religion with a rather honest kind of cynical brutality. He tells us in plain words that "superior strength is the equivalent of superior merit;" in other words, it *is* "superior merit;" and referring to Ireland and her rights, forsooth, he says :—

"There neither is nor can be an inherent privilege in any person or set of persons to live unworthily at their own wills, when they can be led or driven into more honourable courses; and the rights of man—if such rights there be—are not to liberty, but to wise direction and control "—that is, control by us English. There is another passage which I like even better—

"The consent of man was not asked when he was born into the world; his consent will not be asked when his time comes to die. As little has his consent to do with the laws which, while he lives, he is bound to obey. Let a nation be justly governed "—that is, by us English.

As for the Catholic Church in Ireland, the only defect he finds in the course of English policy is, that there was not persecution violent enough and constant enough exercised upon that Church. Here are his words—

"No Government need keep terms with such a creed when there is power to abolish it. To call the repression of opinions which had issued so many times in blood and revolt by the name of religious persecution, is mere abuse of words, while at the same time the best minds in England really believed that, besides its treasonable aspects, the Roman Catholic religion was intellectually degrading and spiritually poisonous."

These, you observe, were not the worst minds in England, but the best; and the Historian most heartily agrees with them. But the author is not altogether averse from "reconciling the loyal priests and the Government, and subsidizing a power which had proved too strong to be violently overthrown." He also cites with approbation the words of a pamphlet which seems one of his favourite authorities—

"Possibly it might be a good plan to abolish the payment of dues, offerings, and fees from the poor Papists to the priests, and settle salaries for them. Their interests would then be closely tied to those of the State, and they might be managed like cannons, whose mouths are still pointed as they please who fill their bellies."

The reader has now a clear enough idea of the high qualifications of this Historian to do the Queen's business in Ireland.

The adventurers under Henry II. came to "take charge" of the Irish, says this Historian, in his preliminary chapter. "The Normans," he assures us, were a people "whose peculiar mission was to govern men;" and it seems they could not help it. Who can resist his fate?—

"They were born rulers of men, and were forced, by the same necessity which has brought the decrepit kingdoms of Asia under the authority of England and Russia, to take the management, eight centuries ago, of the anarchic nations of Western Europe."

It was hard on the Norman people! For these poor devoted rulers of men were forced "by the same necessity," to do much forgery, perjury, and murder, to carry out their missioned task. Neither will our rulers of men altogether give us up when we escape from under their clutch: their care and sympathy follow us round the world. Here, for example, the Irish-Americans who have been living on good enough terms with native American and other citizens, and who have been doing much honest work here, making themselves independent, marrying and giving in marriage, procreating a good breed, which is to have its full share in the labour and the thought and the honourable effort of every kind upon this Continent in the future—these Irish-Americans find themselves followed, even here, from time to time, by agents and emissaries of those blessed governors of men, whose task is to lower us in the eyes of our fellow-citizens, and to make them understand that we are not fit to be trusted as citizens of this or any other country. These English have taken direction of our people, once for all, and cannot without a pang give up the management of us. Though we take the wings of the morning and flee to the uttermost ends of the earth, even there will their hand lead us and their right hand guide us! Even here we find at every turn a vigilant English "ruler of men" cooling our friends, heating our enemies, carefully warning our neighbours that we are false, treacherous, cowardly, and cruel; that we never knew what to do with our own country, when we had one, and will surely do what in us lies to ruin America as we ruined Ireland.

I cannot but admire the Historian when in one of his lectures he comes to deal with the apparently simple suggestion that, inasmuch as England has shown nothing but imbecility and stupidity in her dealings with Ireland for seven hundred years, and has brought the island to be a world's wonder for its long agony of misery, famine, and discontent, she had better, perhaps, relieve herself of the charge, and leave Ireland alone. At this idea he breaks out into a foam of rage. What! let Ireland govern herself! No, never! Anything but that. England will never consent either to Home Rule, or to any altered arrangement which might put Ireland into the way of being able to extort Home Rule—never, until England is beaten to her knees : *never ! never !*

Bravo! First Historian. Beaten to her knees, quotha? Beaten to her mouth and nose must she be. It is precisely the sentiment which I have myself often written and uttered. The British Empire must utterly perish, that is, be dismembered as an empire—or " Ireland must die a daily death, and suffer an endless martyrdom."

Mr Froude seems to admit all this: confesses with a charming ingenuousness that Ireland has been always not only unjustly and cruelly, but stupidly governed by England; that she is now so governed, and is likely to be; nay, that Ireland has ample provocation and perfect right to take up arms and establish her independence on the field. Very well then, says the Historian, draw your sword and *come on !* This is a curiously happy sarcasm, addressed to a nation carefully disarmed by law, and whose houses are at all times subject to search for any kind of weapon. A gang of robbers seizes a traveller, ties him to a tree, disarms him, strips him, robs him of his money; he cries out and remonstrates ; calls them a pack of rascals, demands to be let loose : but one of the brigands replies to him, " Friend, you have no right to liberty unless you fight for it. Your arguments are good, are unanswerable: therefore will you fight us all, there as you stand, with your hands tied behind your back to that tree. If you cannot do this, stop your vain arguments and ' blatant' howlings—enough to disgust the very owls in the trees." As Dean Swift said concerning the book of Molyneux—"In reason, all government, without the consent of the governed, is the very definition of slavery; but, *in fact*, eleven men, well armed, will certainly subdue one single man in his shirt."

Here, then, is the whole political theory and principle of the Historian. We have you down, throttled, stripped, disarmed, garrotted; our treatment of you and of your country has been stupid, and a scandal: it is going to be in the future what it has been in the past: and now what are you going to do about it? I must confess that I like this Crusader of the Period for so honest an exposition of his principles; and feel inclined to take his part against the savage, word-catching critics who have been finding him guilty of misquotations, mistranslations, and even ignorant blunders, as they fondly dream.

And does a citizen of Brooklyn, indeed, or that keen Scotchman, Mr Hosack, or the *Quarterly Review*, and "fifty others," do they, or does any of them, innocently imagine that they can corner the First Living Historian, by pointing out misquotations, falsified authorities, and the like? The Historian defies them. He has composed his "History of England" from "perhaps two hundred thousand documents," and, with a calm irony, invites his critics to follow him through those two hundred thousand pigeon-holes, some in the British Museum, some in the State Paper Office, some in Trinity College Library, or elsewhere; and he cannot think of replying to any special charge of fraud or forgery, unless his accusers go through all those references. "I have read everything myself," he observes in his last lecture. "I have made my own extracts from papers which I might never see a second time." And again—"It often happens that half a letter is in one collection and half in another. There will be two letters from the same person and the same place, on the same subject and on the same day. One may be among the State Papers, another in the British Museum. I will not say that passages from two such letters may not at times appear in my text as if they were one." But he has done his utmost, as he assures us, to tell the truth. And those who doubt it have only to go through his 200,000 pigeon-holes. Thus a rabbit squats at one of the burrows of his intricate warren, and invites the terriers to chase; they give chase; there are a thousand galleries, corridors, labyrinths, the rabbit's ears are seen for a moment peeping at one of the holes; the dog goes for him, but in the twinkling of an eye the rabbit's *fud* is seen at another hole forty yards off.   No straightforward terrier can follow him up, though a well-trained ferret might.   Thus, when the Historian brandishes before us the 200,000 authorities, which we must master before we can "convict" him of even one error, he intimidates the simple mind.   In vain the citizen of Brooklyn points out that the Historian has printed a letter as from Randolph, in Edinburgh, which was never written by said Randolph, attributing to Queen Mary of Scotland an atrocious and blood-thirsty saying. He replies that if Randolph, in Edinburgh, did not write that letter, yet another man somewhere in England did write another letter, and although that *other* letter does not attribute the blood-thirsty utterance to Queen Mary at all, yet the Historian denies that he has been *convicted*—no, only accused by the citizen of Brooklyn.   If he answered the citizen he would have to answer "fifty others"—so many are the charges which have been made against him, and with a frank and noble candour he offers to submit the examination of his authorities to a commission of five Irish judges (out of twelve), with the Irish Lord Chancellor to preside ; they are to examine the 200,000 authorities, and if they find that he has been unfaithful in citing any one, he will expunge that passage.   Can a candid Historian do more?

Some persons may term this proposal an illusory kind of challenge : because the human mind is incapable of conceiving the Lord Chancellor of Ireland and four of the Judges quitting the bench, where they have their own business to mind, flinging off wigs and ermine, burying themselves for (let us say) seven years in the crypts of record-offices, museums and college libraries, closely following the Historian as he fits his references or parts of them to an MS. in London, then dives and re-appears in Dublin to find the other lines of the letter.   Not seven years, but seventeen would be needful for this labour, and the enemies of our First Historian will be sure to say that he never would have proposed such an inquiry but that he knows it to be impossible.   I suggest, then, that he add to the list of commissioners the name of General Grant.

In short, the Historian is too hard a nut for these word-catching critics to crack. Let them not imagine that they can impale such a man as this upon the horn of an inverted comma, or hang him at the tail of a semicolon. It is in vain for the citizen of Brooklyn, or fifty others to taunt him with misquotations; he smiles in front of his 200,000 pigeon holes, and says to them, " Come on, then, gentlemen, follow ! follow!—or send on the Lord Chancellor or the President; either do this or for ever hold your peace." It is in vain also that another small critic points out how the First Historian, having occasion to refer to the oil-bottle of Rheims, speaks of the bottle as a man, and calls him "Saint Ampoul." Do they think they have caught him here? Vain dream! Mr Froude *connait son Rabelais*, and knows that famous voyage which Pantagruel made to consult the Oracle of the *Holy Bottle*, whose name was Bac-Buc; and this is the very saint and the very bottle which the learned person means. Ah! critics, you are not going to trip up the First Living Historian in this flimsy kind of way!

I am now in good humour with the Crusader of the Period, and in the next chapter shall come closer to him.

CHAPTER II.

CONSPIRACY AGAINST THE "FIRST HISTORIAN."

FROUDE is really a man to be congratulated, or almost envied. He has stirred up hosts of vindictive enemies on both sides of the Atlantic. He is the Hero of Two Worlds, in another sense than the Lafayette sense. Like bloodhounds, they are upon his track in either hemisphere; his new book—" The English in Ireland in the Eighteenth Century," will have a sale unexampled: and this—as they say in New England—this is the calculation.

I said that the discussion raised by the Crusader is only beginning. Now it grows hotter and fiercer every day. Not only that fell critic, the bull-dog "Citizen of Brooklyn," holds our Historian fast, with a grip like death, but I find that Mr Prendergast, author of the "Cromwellian Settlement," has fallen upon Historian Froude with a fury even more ferocious than Mr Meline's own; not counting the long array of his other enemies in England and Scotland. I have the honour to make him my compliments. Nothing could fall out more happily for him than this *view-hallo* and full cry of eager hunters. Mr Prendergast, after having read the first volume of the new book, has addressed several letters to the Dublin press; one of which opens thus—

"Mr Froude, I believe, is lighting a fire that he has little conception of. Deep as our hatred has hitherto been at our unparalleled historic wrongs, it is as nothing to the intense detestation we shall hereafter hold the English in. Though the vile English press are unwilling to commit themselves to the support of Mr Froude's crusade against the exiled Irish, until they see the success of it, it is easy to perceive how they sympathise with it, and how gladly they would see the Americans hate us as deeply as they do themselves. For, in

truth, the self-imposed mission of this friend and lover of
Ireland (God save us from our English lovers!) is to turn the
Americans against us."

Here Mr Prendergast is quite wrong, on one point! Our
Historian knew very well that he was lighting a fire; and
intended it. Moreover, he will get out of it himself without
singing a whisker by means of a patent fire-escape which he
has invented. But now, some one may ask, who is Mr
Prendergast? He is an author of whom Mr Froude himself
made honourable mention in this very book, the " English
in Ireland." He says:—

"I cannot pass over this part of my narrative without
making my acknowledgments to Mr Prendergast, to whose
personal courtesy I am deeply indebted, and to whose impar-
tiality and candour in his volume on the Cromwellian Settlement I can offer no higher praise than by saying that the
perusal of it has left on my mind an impression precisely
opposite to that of Mr Prendergast himself. He writes as an
Irish patriot—I as an Englishman; but the difference between
us is not on the facts, but on the opinion to be formed about
them." Meaning that, in Prendergast's opinion, it was hard
measure to compel all Irish land-owners in three of the four
provinces, on a certain day in winter, by sound of trumpet and
beate of drumme, to arise and transplant themselves into the
wilds of Connaught;—but that in Froude's opinion it was a
wholesome measure, intended for the good of the Irish themselves. But what I specially desire to call attention to, in
this place, is the excessive discourtesy with which Mr
Prendergast repays that honourable mention by the First of
Living Historians. After having, by his " personal courtesy,"
(and something more than that) earned so grateful and grace-
ful an acknowledgment from so grand a prince of literature,
this Irishman no sooner reads the book in which so flattering
a notice of himself is contained, than he suddenly turns rough
and rude, and even brutally barbarous. He ignores entirely
the compliment to himself; and is perhaps ashamed of it.
" The twistings and wrigglings of this English viper "—such
is about the best language he can find for his *quondam*
acquaintance. Mr Prendergast admits that he did guide the
researches of our Historian, and did furnish him with authori-

ties and references, sometimes directly, sometimes through others. But he soon had reason to doubt the good faith of this ardent historic investigator, and thought it needful to deal with him accordingly. In the first quarter of the eighteenth century, about the years 1719 and 1723, occurred certain legislative proceedings in the Colonial Parliament of Dublin, concerning which some doubts arose; and both Mr Prendergast and Mr Froude were at the same moment labouring in record offices to ascertain the facts, and discover the documents. Mr Prendergast found what was wanted;—I do not enter here into the odious and indecent details; but must do so before I have done with Froude. Having lighted upon the documents, the laborious Irish scholar, in all good faith, thought he was bound to communicate them to Mr Froude. Here is his own account of this matter in his late letter to the Irish journals :—

"Now for Mr Froude's treatment of this event. He knew he could not avoid it, or mis-state it, as he has done so many other events. For, having met Mr Froude shortly afterwards, making his searches in the State Paper Department at Dublin Castle, I thought it right to tell him of my discovery. But he was already aware, so he told me, of the fact, having seen the original letter in the Public Record Office, London. There was something, however, so extraordinary in the man's demeanour that I had my misgivings that he intended to *misdeal* with the transaction in some way; so I published it in the *Freeman's Journal* of the 28th April, 1871. I confess I had great curiosity to see how he would treat the matter in these circumstances."

The writer then reprints some words and phrases from this book, and continues—

"Let it be remembered that I had bound him with such strong cords by publishing the entire letter beforehand that there was no possibility of his mis-stating the terms or the scope of it; and then observe the writhings and twistings of this English viper, that, nursed in his youthful sickness by the poor peasantry of Mayo, and since that day a frequent visitor to Ireland, seeks to spit his venom against us at home by publishing this book, and then immediately rushes to America to endeavour to instil into the English race abroad the same hatred he and his colleagues are filled with at home."

I mean to tell something of the matter which was in question, before I have done; but in the meantime it is enough to arouse the sympathies of all readers in favour of Mr Froude, by showing the shocking manner in which his kindly overtures to Prendergast have been received. It is true no compliment from our Historian could elevate the reputation of Mr Prendergast, the author of the most perfect Monograph of one special and cardinal point in our Irish history; but still it seems hard that the recipient of so pretty a compliment should have no better return to make than refusing the courtesy with both his hands, saying—" Keep off, you English viper ! " Is the time indeed come when these generous tributes from one literary man to another, which give such a grace and charm to the intercourse of lofty intellects, are to become of no account? Is a gentleman, who has received so flattering an eulogy from a great man, justified in responding with a kick and a curse? Let a discerning public judge.

In the midst of all this tumult of abuse the First Historian walks serene; he is altogether impassive, going calmly on the even tenor of his way, answering all hostile critics with disdain. Mr Meline has vainly tried to worry him into giving some sign, making some defence in the matter of Queen Mary of Scotland and her " latest Historian." Yet the critic seems to have been aware from the first that he would get nothing out of the man. Says that inevitable citizen of Brooklyn :—

" That Mr Froude at this or at any other time would answer the charges presented in ' Mary Queen of Scots and her latest English Historian,' I have never expected. He cannot do it and better his position, and I am, moreover, sufficiently familiar with his ' manner of fence ' with critics at home to know that he would not now attempt serious responses in a case of any gravity. Mr Froude cannot reply to my allegations, because he says, ' I am on one side of the Atlantic, and my books and papers are on the other;' and he then repeats the plaintive wail, made several years ago in the *Pall Mall Gazette*, touching his gigantic labours with documents and MSS. ' in half-a-dozen languages.' But during all the years Mr Froude was at home among his books and papers, his most aggressive critics and those of bluntest speech succeeded no better than I have in obtaining answer, explanation, or apology from him. In reply to the most damaging imputations, to the most offensive accusations, he had nothing to say—and, wisely, said nothing."

It is an attitude of grand disdain; but this inevitable Meline does not like it; he would prefer that the Historian would be good enough to explain some of those very numerous passages in which he has brought forward misquotations or palmed off mistranslations, and to expound how it has happened that *all* those "clerical errors," as Froude calls them, were on one side, always going to favour the scoundrel he intended to whitewash, and to blacken the unhappy Papist he meant to cover with obloquy.

Father Burke, I think, in his lectures, only ventured to call in question one citation of an authority made by his opponent —a statement that, while the Americans were in revolt, the Irish Catholics, represented by Lord Fingal and others, went crawling to the foot of the throne, praying to be led against the rebellious Americans. The great Dominican said he had searched for some such address, thinking very naturally that a document of so much importance would certainly have been printed; but he had not found any document answering the description, although he had found, in Curry's Collection, an address testifying general loyalty. It is servile enough, God knows, and is signed certainly *Fingal, Gormanstown, Dillon, Kenmare,* and many others; but it says no word of America. Here is the Historian's proud rejoinder in his last lecture:—

"I quoted a loyal address to George the Third, signed in the name of the whole body by the leading Irish Catholics. Father Burke says that, though fulsome in its tone, it contains no words about America. As he meets me with a contradiction, I can but insist that *I copied* the words which I read to you from the original in the State Paper Office, and I will read one or two sentences of it again. The address declares that the Catholics of Ireland abhorred the unnatural rebellion against His Majesty which had broken out among his American subjects; that they laid at his feet 2,000,000 loyal, faithful, and affectionate hearts and hands, ready to exert themselves against His Majesty's enemies in any part of the world; that their loyalty had been always as the dial to the sun, true though not shone upon."

This last line—is the Historian very certain that it is not a quotation from Tom Moore? At any rate, he peremptorily shuts all mouths by saying, "I can but *insist* that I copied it in the State Paper Office." Now, the fact is, that nobody, by this time, believes one word that the First of Living Historians writes or utters, upon his own authority. There are, accordingly, many still who will not believe that such a document exists—not at least until after the Lord Chancellor of Ireland and the Judges have exhibited a certified copy of it, in the Chancery Office, Four Courts, Dublin.

With his head high, and lofty disdain upon his countenance, this haughty creature thus finally brushes off the troublesome swarm of his assailants, and wraps himself nobly in his mantle of proof. Closing his last lecture, he says:—

"Here I must leave him" (namely, Father Burke). "I leave untouched a large number of blots which I had marked for criticism; but if I have not done enough to him already, I shall waste my words with trying to do more; and for the future, as long as I remain in America, neither he, if he returns to the charge, nor any other assailant, must look for further answer from me. His own knowledge of his subject is wide and varied; but I can compare his workmanship to nothing so well as to one of the lives of his own Irish saints, in which legend and reality are so strangely blended that the true aspects of things and character can no longer be discerned."

The sarcasm about the Irish Saint is in English good taste, being addressed to an Irish Dominican Friar! The Christian Young Men rub their hands with glee, over so neat and cunning a cut administered to those superstitious Romanists. Yet, after all, perhaps the Historian has not spent much of his time in studying the lives of the Irish Saints. He is more deeply read in the legend of that round-bellied French saint, the jolly "St Ampoul;" where, perhaps, Father Burke cannot follow him.

The main thing which we learn most explicitly from this last paragraph is, that the malignant critics of the Historian may now consider themselves safe from the effects of his resentment. There are fifty of them; and I am now emboldened to become the fifty-first: he will not notice any of us; his sole reply to one and all-being "*Dixi.*" Very well; although I should deem it a very high honour indeed; if I could anyhow

goad and badger so illustrious a person into replying, even in
the most damaging manner to *me*, I must not think of so flattering an encounter: and as I have the Book itself before me, I
can only comment upon its text as my lights may enable me.
So now for the Book itself.

At the opening of a "section" of chapter third, the Historian,
speaking of the situation of the country in the reign of James
II., has this frank and satisfactory statement of the position of
affairs—

"The Irish believed *that Ireland was theirs*: that the English
were invading tyrants who had stolen their lands, broken up
their laws and habits, and proscribed their creed. The English
believed that Ireland was a country attached, inseparably, *by
situation and circumstances*, to the English crown; that they
were compelled to govern a people who were unable or unwilling to govern themselves; and that the spoliation with which
they were reproached had been forced upon them by the
treachery and insubordination of the native owners. Between
these two views of the same facts no compromise was possible."

Certainly not; and, indeed, everybody who has any interest
in the question ought to feel obliged to the English Historian
for stating the issue so clearly, and for arguing it so steadily
and consistently throughout his work. Mr Prendergast
expresses the hope that "The English in Ireland" may be
translated and published in France and in Germany, as we may
be sure it will be. In the meantime, we have it in very plain
English; so that Americans (if they care) have the best opportunity of learning the whole case of our nation in its relation
to England, upon excellent authority. I call it excellent
authority *for this special purpose*—namely, for ascertaining the
genuine sentiment of the English people, because all the
author's historical books have an enormous currency in that
country; and this one, above all, is sure to be devoured, by
the multitudinous readers of England, with a greedy delight.
I beg leave to commend it to them. I give my modest aid to
the advertising of it. In truth, if some Irishman, possessed of
the grim humour of Dean Swift, had written these chapters
with the intention of presenting the English case in the most
grotesquely horrible and offensive point of view, he could
scarcely go beyond our Historian. One might be almost

inclined to suspect him of this malignant design, if the man were a wit like the Dean of St Patrick's. But there is not a ray of humour in his intellect : and when he gravely propounds that, to term the "abolishing" of the religion of a people by fines, whipping, transportation, and the gallows, a case of religious persecution is "a mere abuse of words;" and when he mentions as a wholly untenable theory the belief prevalent among the Irish, *that Ireland was theirs*, he means no sarcasm; it is the most serious and stolid British insolence ; not intended to be laughed at by any means, nor a fit subject for amusement at all. The thing has an odour of blood. Such words call up the ghosts of many generations of murdered men; and they are intended, and calculated, to make more such ghosts for ages yet to come. If I have heretofore spoken of this man's performances in a tone somewhat like levity, I drop that tone from the present moment, and proceed to expose the Historian in all his naked horror.

There is no need for the present purpose to examine this writer's account of the "occupation of Ireland," at the end of the twelfth century, by people whom he calls the Normans, "whose peculiar mission was to govern men." The conquerors of England, and the invaders of Ireland, were, according to the Historian, not only Normans but Norman aristocrats. In this, as in everything else, he carefully consults and flatters the prevailing sentiment of his own people at the present day. The English cannot endure to say, or to hear, that their island was conquered in one battle by a mob of *Frenchmen*—Frenchmen, pure and simple, including those who lived in Normandy. They cannot endure to be told that one whole wing, and one-third of William's army, consisted of Bretons; another wing of Gascons and other people of the south and centre of France. And as for the "Normans" who came over afterwards, "to take charge" of Ireland, it seems to our English friends invidious to dwell upon the fact that they were not Normans at all—you might as well call them Auvergnats or Savoyards. The Fitzstephens and Fitzmaurices, who preceded Henry the Second, were Geraldines, the Italian Gherardini; and their mother was the notorious Nesta, a Welsh lady of no uneasy virtue. Out of the same nest as Nesta came also Giraldus Cambrensis, the very first of the carpet-bag school of writers upon Ireland. And when Henry himself came over with his knights, he also had no title to be called a Norman aristocrat, nor a Norman at all —for, in fact, he was born in Anjou, where his father before him was born, and his children after him. He became, indeed, Duke of Normandy, and he became King of England; yet he never called himself a Norman; and if any one had affronted him by calling him an Englishman, he would have had the insulter lashed with dog-whips.

I notice this rubbish about "Norman rulers of men," only to point out how sedulously the Historian has consulted the national vanity of his public; but I shall now apply myself to his treatment of that which he calls "the gravest event in all Irish history, the turning-point on which all later controversies between England and Ireland hinge"—The "Massacre" of 1641.

"Those who see in that massacre the explanation and the defence of the subsequent treatment of Ireland, however unwilling to revive the memory of scenes which rivalled in carnage the horrors of St Bartholomew, are compelled to repeat the evidence once held to be unreasonable." In these words (page 83) the Historian commits himself to the whole ghastly story. He will not, indeed, insist that two hundred thousand Protestants were assassinated in six months. But if there was a certain exaggeration in the estimate of the numbers, he assures us that "for these enormous figures the Catholic priests were responsible. They returned the numbers of the killed in their several parishes, up to March, 1642, as 154,000." Also, "Sir John Temple considered that 150,000 perished in two months, or 300,000 in two years." But as our learned Historian knows well enough that there were not so many Protestants in all Ireland, counting women and children, he thinks it best to take the cooler and calmer estimate of Lord Clarendon, who reduced the estimate to 40,000, or he is willing even to take Sir William Petty's numbers, namely, 37,000. And even these figures, he says, may "seem too large." But that there was in fact a most frightful massacre perpetrated in Ulster, he feels it his duty to reaffirm; and for proof of it, in all its details, he refers to the folio volumes of sworn depositions now to be read in the library of Trinity College, "whose evidence is the eternal witness of blood which the Irish Catholics have, from that time to this, been vainly trying to wash away."

Now, I propose to show—

First, that there was no massacre at all.

Second, that the Historian knows there was no massacre.

Third, that he intentionally and advisedly cites "authorities" which prove nothing and shed not a ray of light.

Fourth, that in producing Temple, Petty, Dean Maxwell, and others, as witnesses, he is producing those carpet-baggers who had need of establishing a "massacre," because it was their title-deed to the great estates afterwards confiscated—that, in short, there was *money in the massacre.*

Fifth, that he has woven together this tissue of sanguinary falsehood for the purpose of blackening and scandalising a whole people before the civilised world, or, as he expresses it, making that gory fable " the explanation and defence of the subsequent treatment of Ireland," meaning Penal Laws, and the whipping-post and the gallows and universal plunder of all persons who went to Mass.

Sir William Petty gathered together, out of the confiscated estates, those vast domains which his descendant, Lord Lansdowne, now possesses in Ireland. Sir John Temple was the founder of the Irish fortunes of the Temples Lords Palmerston. Dr Maxwell was made Bishop of Kilmore, in reward for one affidavit; to be sure it was a hard one, as we shall see; but he swallowed it, and it agreed with him. Sir John Borlase, an Englishman, but a carpet-bag judge on the Irish bench, had a share out of the spoil of the Papists. And these men and many others like them, and their dependants, could not afford to let the "massacre" be questioned at all; it was on the massacre they lived and were providing for their little families; if any man at that time doubted the massacre they would have his blood.

Indeed, in the last lecture of the Historian, he refers to the Rev. Ferdinando Warner, a very respectable clergyman of the Church of England, and author of a History of Ireland, who made a most careful examination into the alleged murders of Protestants, and reduces them to two thousand one hundred people—a heavy hecatomb enough, one might think: but it will not answer our Historian's purpose at all: he cannot come down to so low a figure : he does not know but that the next Protestant may whittle it down to nothing. So he treats Mr Warner's estimate with a pooh pooh, and actually says (I quote the *World's* very good report), "I am sorry to say I have known many Protestants entirely unable to distinguish truth from falsehood." Indeed, the Historian is utterly disgusted at such a " Protestant " as this, who tries to cut and lop away the whole foundation on which the treatment of Ireland is grounded and justified. Such a Protestant is no better than that Papist keeper of records in London who actually answered Mr Meline's inquiry by giving him such information as convicted the Historian of fraud.

I am about to prove myself a very poor sort of Protestant, according to the Historian's religious test : for the task I have undertaken and the end I have set before me are to demonstrate, to all rational and fair-minded people, that this individual, purporting to be a historian, has, both by his lectures and his book, deliberately falsified the very history which he undertook to elucidate ; that he has used his researches of years with the cold malignity of a spider to involve his intended victim in an inextricable network of black falsehood ; referring for his "facts" to authorities he knew to be worse than worthless ; presenting those pretended authorities to his readers as trustworthy and undeniable ; suppressing, in general, or else disparaging (as of no consequence) all evidence which bore against his bloody plan ; and that he has done all this with a certain " purpose fixed as the stars "—to use a fine expression of his own ; but, in fact, I prefer my own illustration to his, my own spider to his star :—and that this settled purpose was, to cover with execration, and to overwhelm with a load of calumny, a generation of men, all dead two or three hundred years ago, in such sort as to cast a shadow of horror over their children and their children's children, even to the ninth and tenth generation. I know it may be suggested that the motive of his labour was, perhaps, no worse than to insure a vast circulation for his Book, by flattering the conceit of his own people, and feeding their bitterest and dearest national passion. Let those who find this a good excuse give to the Historian all the benefit of it.

CHAPTER III.

MAKING THE ISSUE.

I SHALL have little or nothing to say touching the cruel oppressions inflicted, for so many ages, upon my countrymen; and absolutely nothing at all in the way of complaint or vituperation, on account of those sad events. Let it be granted, for the present, that the English, or the Normans, or whoever the Historian pleases, were "forced by circumstances to take charge" of Ireland, and that, having so taken charge, they were forced to take all the lands of the island for their own people; forced to proscribe the religion of the country, and transport priests for saying Mass; forced to stir up continual insurrections in order to help the good work of confiscation; let all this theory stand admitted; but whatever may be thought of all that, the present point which I shall make is, that the Historian bears false witness at any rate—Historian and History being all one huge fraud together. If I do not prove this, I prove nothing.

Taking up, then, the said History at the "turning-point" of the famous "Massacre," I shall first give some account of the array of witnesses brought forward to establish it; and especially of Temple, Borlase, and Petty, and of the "forty folios" of depositions; testimonies, indeed, which I did not expect that any Englishman, or any Orangeman, would ever have the audacity to cite again. As the First of Living Historians, however, has thought proper to drag to light again the whole hideous romance, and has actually come over to America to pour it into the horrified ears of this people—both by lectures and through the medium of a book—I shall now follow him into the revolting details at least of the one period of a few years which he has selected as the turning-point in the history of my native country.

It is very observable, indeed, and somewhat entertaining, that from his very dark portraiture of the Irish people in general, he kindly excepts us *Protestants*. "When I call them a generation of riotous and treacherous cut-throats," he says, "I don't mean *you*. You Protestants, on the contrary, are the noble and godly element, which we, the English, have introduced, to bring some order out of that bloody chaos—you are the missioned race—as Macaulay, the predecessor of Froude, calls you—the *imperial race* that we have planted, enabling you to help yourselves to all the lands and goods of the irreclaimable Popish savages, that you might hold the fair island in trust for us—for *us*, Ireland's masters, and yours. You are our own 'Protestant Boys:' I pat you on the back, and exhort you not to do the work of the Lord negligently." But I am not myself acquainted with any Irish Protestant gentleman who is likely to accept graciously this considerate exception in our favour. My own friends in Ireland, from boyhood—at school—at the University, and in after life —have been generally of opinion that it would be a blessed and glorious deed to sweep into the sea the last remnants of English domination in their country. I never was taught in my youth that the man of Two Sacraments has a natural right and title to take all the possessions, and to take the lives, of the men of Seven Sacraments. My father was not only a Protestant, but a Protestant clergyman; and he, in the year '98, when only a student in college, was sworn in as an United Irishman; and then proceeded to swear in his friends; and the noble object of that society was to abolish the English power in Ireland. Grattan was a Protestant, and he declared that he despised the pretended liberty of half a million of his countrymen, based upon the serfdom and slavery of two millions more: and it was this Protestant who penned the Declaration of Irish Independence, and created a Volunteer army to make good his words. And Tone was a Protestant, who brought on two invasions of the French, to free his native island from the English. And Tandy was a Protestant, who commanded the artillery of the Volunteer army. I fear that the Historian will find, in our Protestants, an ungrateful set of clients. We will not have his advocacy upon any terms. I can imagine that I see William Smith O'Brien receiving the courtesies of our Historian, as a Protestant, and therefore, a sort of deputy Briton. This revered name of O'Brien I cannot mention without bowing in homage to so grand a memory. For years we broke the bitter bread of exile together, and drank of the same cup of captivity. He lived for the cause of his country's independence, and never till his latest breath repented of his gallant though fruitless effort to destroy with armed hand the tyranny that was gnawing away his people's life. It would be easy to name many other Protestants of the same principles; but at present let us content ourselves with Mr Prendergast, who has so fiercely declined the special compliment offered him by this Historian. And, in truth, the very best book upon the subject of the turning-point of Irish History is this very " Cromwellian Settlement," by Prendergast. Let nobody take Froude's poison without taking Prendergast's antidote.

That there was an insurrection is certain. It began on the 23rd of October, in the year 1641; and the whole plan and purpose of it were to retake and possess the farms and houses which had been forcibly taken away from the Irish of Ulster, only a few years before. From twenty years to thirty years had elapsed since most of the people of six counties had been driven to the mountains and bogs, that their pleasant fields might be occupied by Scotch and English settlers. The remnant of those Ulster clans had been reduced to the condition of labourers, or very small cottiers. Many men of high name, with the culture and associations of the gentry of that day, were tilling, as ploughmen, and reaping as harvest men, for the stranger, fields that had been their own. Others, with their shivering families, could look down from the brow of Tyrone hills upon those smiling valleys of the Blackwater and the Foyle, whence their own fathers had trooped, forty years before, to join their clans on the Blackwater, and to ride beside the bridle-rein of Hugh O'Neill, at the Yellow Ford. Of this sad and plundered people many of the young and high-spirited had emigrated to France or Spain, to take service in the armies of those countries. The rest lingered sorrowfully, in the hope that some alteration might be brought about, in their doleful lot, by a change of kings. For example, when King Charles the First came to the throne of England, there seemed to them a prospect of some share of relief or reparation:

in the meantime they endured life, hiding their clergy in woods and caves, concealing themselves with their wives and little ones, as much as possible, from the notice of the insolent intruders. And when, at last, that King Charles and his Parliament were on the very point of open war, the leaders of the Northern Irish thought they might give counsel to their people—disarmed and scattered as they were—that the time was come to strike a blow. Of the long series of exasperating provocations which now at last made them ready to try this desperate remedy, I need not here speak. It is enough that the turning-point was reached.

The Historian here cannot bring himself to specify names and dates, nor even to indicate, save in a general way, the authorities for his fearful story. His sensibilities will not permit him to dwell upon scenes so sanguinary; but he gives this general account of the situation :—

"Savage creatures of both sexes, yelping in chorus, and brandishing their skenes; boys practising their young hands in stabbing and torturing the English children—these were the scenes which were witnessed daily through all parts of Ulster. The fury extended even to the farm-stock, and sheep and oxen were slaughtered, not for food, but in the blindness of rage. The distinction between Scots and English soon vanished. Religion was made the new dividing line, and the one crime was to be a Protestant. The escorts proved in most cases but gangs of assassins. In the wildest of remembered winters, the shivering fugitives were goaded along the highways stark naked and foodless. If some, happier than the rest, found a few rags to throw about them, they were torn instantly away. If others, in natural modesty, twisted straw ropes round their waists, the straw was set on fire. When the tired little ones dropped behind, the escort lashed the parents forward, and the children were left to die. One witness, Adam Clover, of Slonory, in Cavan, swore that he saw a woman who had been thus deserted, set upon by three Irish women, who stripped her naked in frost and snow. She fell in labour under their hands, and she and her child died. Many were buried alive. Those who died first were never buried, but were left to be devoured by dogs, and rats, and swine. Some were driven into rivers, and drowned, some hanged, some mutilated, some ripped with knives. The priests told the people 'that the Protestants were worse than dogs; they were devils, and served the devil; and the killing of them was a meritorious act.' One wretch stabbed a woman with a baby in her arms, and left the infant in mockery on its dead mother's breast, bidding it 'Suck, English bastard.' The insurgents swore in their madness they would not leave English man, woman, or child alive in Ireland. They flung babies into boiling pots, or tossed them into the ditches to the pigs. They put out grown men's eyes, turned them adrift to wander, and starved them to death. Two cow-boys boasted of having murdered thirty women and children; and a lad was heard swearing that his arm was so tired with killing, that he could scarce lift his hand above his head."

The main authority for all this is Sir John Temple, whose story is founded upon the famous folios of Depositions; but the Historian does not cite the depositions themselves, merely saying that they are the "eternal witness of blood." To those who have made Irish history a study, these wonderful affidavits are familiar, and I should be ashamed to take up space with them, but that to most readers they will be something new, and will, besides, show the exact sources from which the Historian has drawn his bloody marvels. Here, for example, are several specimens—

"The examination of Dame Butler, who being duly sworn, deposeth that

"*She was credibly informed by Dorothy Renals*, who had been several times an eye-witness of these lamentable spectacles, that she had seen to the number of five-and-thirty English going to execution; and that she had seen them when they were executed, their bodies exposed to devouring ravens, and not afforded as much as burial.

"And this deponent saith, That *Sir Edward Butler did credibly inform her* that James Butler of Finyhinch had hanged and put to death *all the English that were at Goran and Wells, and all thereabouts* ! ! !

"Jane Jones, servant to the deponent, did see the English formerly specified going to their execution, and, as she conceived, they were about the number of thirty-five; *and was told by Elizabeth Home* that there were forty gone to execution. Jurat. Sept. 7, 1642. ANNE BUTLER."

C

"Thomas Fleetwood, late curate of Kilbeggan, in the county of Westmeath, deposeth, That *he hath heard from the mouths of the rebels themselves of great cruelties acted by them.* And, for one instance, that they stabbed the mother, one Jane Addis by name, and left her little suckling child, not a quarter old, by the corpse, and then they put the breast of its dead mother into its mouth, and bid it ' *suck, English bastard,*' and so left it there to perish."

"Richard Bourk, bachelor in divinity, of the county of Fermanagh, deposeth, That *he heard, and verily believeth,* the burning and killing of one hundred, at least, in the Castle of Tullah; and that the same was done after fair quarter promised. Jurat. July 12, 1643."

In looking through the monstrous farrago of swearing, it is remarkable, first, that scarcely any one saw the horrid deeds he or she swears to, but only tells what somebody told somebody else, who told this deponent; also, that in most cases the authorities for the statements are called, in general terms, "the rebels." For example—

"Katherine, the relict of William Coke, of the county of Armagh, deposeth, That many of her neighbours, who had been prisoners among the rebels, *said and affirmed that divers of the rebels would confess, brag, and boast* how they took an English Protestant, one Robert Wilkinson, at Kilmore, and held his feet in the fire until they burned him to death."

To do the Historian justice, there is not one of the fearful scenes he has above described that he did not find in evidence daily sworn to upon the Holy Evangelists. The babies flung into boiling pots, or left to be devoured by swine; the men and women stripped naked, and driven out under the wild winter weather. Nay, more, he is too modest, and does not cite by any means the most revolting cases, fearing, perhaps, to give a certain grotesque air to his pages. I can supply him, for his second edition, with more and better horrors. Stripping, for instance, is but a trifle; why not give us the case of Margaret Fermeney, an old woman of seventy-five, who swears that on her way up to Dublin, "she was stripped naked by the Irish *seven times* in one day." He will find this in the famous folios, and also in Temple. Or why not tell us what Elizabeth Baskerville swears she heard a murderer's wife say to the murderer, her husband—

"Elizabeth Baskerville deposeth, That *she heard the wife of Florence Fitz-Patrick, find much fault with her husband's soldiers*, because they did not bring along with them the grease of Mrs Nicholson, whom they had slain, for her to make candles withal. Jurat.· April 26, 1643."

Indeed, several of the affidavits make express mention of the strong desire those Irish had to collect Protestant grease. And it is all set forth in those volumes, which are the "eternal witness of blood!"

I observe that the Historian has avoided the many miracles and ghost stories which are found in the same repertory of facts. Yet these would greatly heighten the sensational charm of his work; and here is one which might probably suit him.

"Arthur Culm, of Clonghwater, in the county of Cavan, esquire, deposeth, That *he was credibly informed*, by some that were present there, that there were thirty women and young children and seven men flung into the river of Belturbert; and when some of them offered to swim for their lives, they were, by the rebels, followed in boats, and knocked on the head with poles; the same day they hanged two women at Turbert; and *this deponent doth verily believe* that Mulmore O'Rely, the then sheriff, had a hand in the commanding the murder of those said persons, *for that he saw him write two notes*, which he sent to Turbert by Brien O'Rely, upon whose coming these murders were committed; and those persons who were present also affirmed that the bodies of *those thirty persons drowned did not appear upon the water till about six weeks after, past; as the said O'Rely came to the town, all the bodies came floating up to the very bridge*; those persons were all formerly stayed in the town by his protection, when the rest of their neighbours in the town went away."

There are many other very miraculous facts sworn to, which are quite accessible to the Historian; also many other and still more savage cruelties, which he does his readers positive wrong in suppressing. I shall present still another *spicilegium* culled from the "eternal witness of blood;" and afterwards explain *why* these depositions were called for, *how* they were obtained, and how they were paid for. All which the learned Historian knew very well, but preferred to suppress for the honour of Protestant human nature.

CHAPTER IV.

THE SWEARERS.

THE seventeenth century was the period of our most thriving Protestant trade in swearing. It was the time of Popish *plots*, and of multitudinous "depositions." As for the thirty-four folio volumes of oaths, to which Historian Froude calmly refers us, as an "eternal witness," that learned person must know that many of them were paid for in money, most of them in confiscated land and lucrative office; that many of them were never sworn at all, appearing with the pen drawn across the words "being first duly sworn;" that the Lords of the Council of Ireland, and the heads of the "English interest" in the island, absolutely needed these oaths for procuring the indictment of all Irish Catholics who owned anything; and that they bought the said oaths as in market overt. Carte, author of the "Life of Ormonde," is a Protestant authority; and Mr Froude has read his work, for he often cites it where it suits him; but he takes care not to give us this passage from Carte's first volume—

"The Roman Catholics complained that *there were strange practices used with the jurors, menaces to some, promises of rewards, and parts of the forfeited estates;* and though great numbers of the indicted persons might be really guilty, *there was too much reason given to suspect the evidence.* I am the more inclined to suspect there was *a good deal of corruption and iniquity in the methods of gaining the indictments,* because I find a very remarkable memorandum made by the Marquis of Ormonde, in his own writing, of a passage in the Council on April 23, 1643. There was then a letter read at the Board, from a person who claimed a great merit to himself in getting some hundreds of gentlemen indicted, and the rather for that he had laid out sums of money to procure witnesses to give evidence to a jury for the finding those indictments. This was an intimate friend of Sir William Parson's, and might very well know that such methods would be approved by him."

The trade in affidavits had begun in 1642, a few months after the insurrection broke out. In the following year, when Ormonde read this letter, there was a perfect deluge of oaths; and the business went on very briskly for several years, until Sir William Petty, who longed to get at the Ormonde estates themselves, used a remarkable expression, as we read in the same Carte—

"Sir William Petty bragged that he had got witnesses who would have sworn through a three-inch board to evict the Duke."

It may perhaps be thought very harsh to blame too much these poor, hard-working swearers. If our good Protestants, driven out of house and home by "the rebels," and, finding that there was a demand for oaths, put their imaginations to the rack, to invent the most horrible tales—the more ghastly the higher price—and hawked them in Dublin to noble lords and honourable gentlemen who would buy, is a forlorn Protestant, who has been stripped bare, to be grudged even the chance of selling his naked soul?

Many of the swearers, indeed, received no cash in hand, but were sure of higher reward; which was the case of Dean Maxwell and other parsons. But, in dealing with the whole mass of evidence, it is curious to observe what caution and discrimination the Historian has shown. He names but two of the swearers. Dean Maxwell and one Adam Clover, and in constructing his general narrative of the atrocities, never hints that most of them are related on hearsay; and he omits altogether those which contain manifest impossibilities, and true Protestant miracles, and especially the *ghosts*.

In the last chapter I mentioned the miracle of the floating corpses on the river at Belturbet, that, after lying drowned six weeks, came up and swam against the stream up to the very bridge, at the moment when Maelmorra O'Reilly entered the village by that bridge. They came up to confront and accuse him of their murder—as a certain person was "credibly informed:" for, in fact, O'Reilly had still an estate in Cavan;

and it was this estate which was guilty of the murder. But these swimming corpses did not speak, in which respect they fall short of the spectres of the Bann. It was said, and repeated several times in depositions, that, "about the 20th of December," (for they seldom give us dates at all, and then in a very loose way,) "the rebels" drowned one hundred and eighty Protestants in the Bann, at Portadown bridge; that this was followed by other *noyades* at the same place, week after week, until, as Dean Maxwell computes, there were over a thousand Protestants drowned there. The widow, Catherine Cooke, not only swears to this, but adds in her affidavit this ghastly fact—

"And that, *about nine days afterwards, she saw a vision or spirit, in the shape of a man,* as she apprehended, that appeared in that river, in the place of the drowning, *bolt upright, breast-high, with hands lifted up, and stood in that posture there, until the latter end of Lent next following;* about which time, some of the English army marching in those parts, whereof her husband was one (*as he and they confidently told this deponent),* saw that spirit or vision standing upright, and in the posture aforementioned; but, after that time, the said spirit or vision vanished, and appeared no more, that she knoweth."

This was not sworn until the 24th of February, 1643, when there was a most urgent demand, and good price, for the most frightful oaths. Other witnesses had a still more inventive imagination; and Elizabeth Price, of Armagh, swears that, on a certain day—

"She went unto the bridge aforesaid, *about twilight in the evening; then and there, upon a sudden, appeared unto them a vision or spirit, assuming the shape of a woman, waist-high, upright in the water, often repeating the word, Revenge! Revenge! Revenge!* whereat this deponent, and the rest, being put into an amazement and affright, walked from the place."

There are five or six other deponents who swear to these shrieking apparitions; but it is time to come to Dean Maxwell, afterwards bishop, that consecrated, anointed and mitred perjurer, whose long affidavit is relied upon with the greatest confidence by Borlase and Temple, and is, therefore, cited by Froude, as a main part of his authorities, but without giving any of the Dean's very words. So it is now necessary to state what this reverend divine swore to.

This affidavit was sworn on August 22nd, 1642, ten months after the insurrection began. The first notable thing in it is the extraordinary habit which "the rebels" had, whenever they had cut a good many throats anywhere, to come running to this Protestant divine to tell him their exploits—

"Deponent saith, That *the rebels themselves told him, this* deponent, that they murdered nine hundred and fifty-four in one morning, in the county of Antrim; and that, besides them, *they supposed* they killed above eleven or twelve hundred more in that county; *they told him likewise,* that Colonel Brian O'Neill killed about a thousand in the county of Down, besides three hundred killed near Killeleigh, and many hundreds, both before and after, in both these counties."

It is even more strange, to find that Sir Phelim O'Neill himself, the very head and front of the "Massacre," whenever he had slaughtered a good herd of Protestants, always made a confidant of our amiable Dean—

"That *he heard Sir Phelim likewise report,* that he killed six hundred English at Garvagh, in the county of Derry; and that he had left neither man, woman, nor child alive in the barony of Munterlony, in the county of Tyrone, and betwixt Armagh and the Newry, in the several plantations and lands of Sir Archibald Atcheson, John Hamilton, Esq., the Lord Caulfield, and the Lord Mountnorris; and saith also, that there were above two thousand of the British murdered for the most part in their own houses, *whereof he was informed by a Scotsman,* who was in those parts with Sir Phelim, and saw their houses filled with their dead bodies. In the Glenwood, towards Dromore, there were slaughtered, *as the rebels told the deponent, upwards of twelve thousand in all,* who were all killed in their flight to the county of Down. The numbers of the people drowned at the bridge of Portadown are diversely reported, according as men staid among the rebels. This deponent, who staid as long as any, and *had better intelligence than* most of the English amongst them, and best reason to know the truth, saith, There were (*by their own report*) one hundred and ninety drowned with Mr Fullerton; at another time they threw one hundred and forty over the said bridge;

at another time, thirty-six or thirty-seven; and so continued drowning more or fewer, for seven or eight weeks, so as the fewest which can be supposed there to have perished must needs be above one thousand, besides as many more drowned between that bridge and the great lough of Montjoy, besides those that perished by the sword, fire, and famine, in Coubrasil (Clanbrassil), and the English plantations adjacent; which, in regard there escaped not three hundred out of all these quarters, must needs amount to many thousands.

"And further saith that he knew one boy that dwelt near unto himself, and not exceeding fourteen years of age, who killed, at Kinnaird, in one night, fifteen able strong men with his skein, they being disarmed, and most of their feet in the stocks."

The reader must remark that this hard-swearing divine does not affirm any of the above matters as of his own knowledge, until he comes to the wicked boy. About this there can be no mistake, for he knew the boy; not that he actually saw the bad boy kill those fifteen able strong men, but perhaps some frightened woman told some other woman, who told the Dean; or probably some of the "rebels" themselves narrated the story to him, for these rebels appear to have had a certain malicious pleasure in "taking a rise out of" the Dean, to use a vulgar Irish expression.

But the reader is not to imagine that the Dean was not himself an eye-witness of anything at all; indeed he was so, for he saw, like Moses and the Israelites, a *pillar of fire*, and he remarked the disloyal silence of the dogs and cocks, as follows:—

"And the deponent further saith, That the first three days and nights of this present rebellion, viz., October, 23, 24, and 25, *it was generally observed that no cock crew, or any dog was heard to bark, no not when the rebels came in great multitudes unto the Protestants' houses by night to rob and murder them;* and about three or four nights before the six and fifty persons were taken out of the deponent's house and drowned, and amongst those the deponent's brother, Lieutenant James Maxwell, in the dark of the moon, about one of the clock at night, *a light was observed, in manner of a long pillar, to shine for a long way through the air, and refracted upon the north gable of the house.*

It gave so great a light, about an hour together, that *divers of
the watch read both letters and books of a very small character
thereby.* The former the deponent knoweth to be most true,
both by his own experience, and the general observation of as
many as the deponent met with in the county Armagh. The
latter was seen by all those of the deponent's family, and
besides by many of his Irish guard."

The zealous divine is next happily enabled to expose a
most cunning device of "the rebels," for the purpose of concealing the extent of the carnage they had committed, and to
make people believe that, after all, they had only assassinated
one hundred and fifty-four thousand (out of 20,000 Protestants
in Ulster) within three or four months.

"And further saith, That it was credibly told him, that the
rebels, *lest they should hereafter be charged with more murders
than they had committed,* commanded their priests to bring in a
true account of them; and that the persons so slaughtered,
whether in Ulster or the whole kingdom, the deponent durst
not inquire, in March last, amounted unto one hundred and
fifty-four thousand."

We shall see this monstrous fable repeated by others,
adopted without scruple by Sir John Temple, embodied in a
letter to the king from the Lords of the Council at Dublin (of
whom Temple was one).

"They murdered, up to the end of March last, of men,
women, and children, 154,000, as is acknowledged by the
priests appointed to collect their numbers."

Of course, Mr Froude eagerly repeated this story, and
dares to say that, if there was any exaggeration in the
numbers, "the Catholic priests were responsible." But the
most singular circumstance is, that nobody ever saw these
"returns" made by the priests; nobody even knows to whom
the returns were made, nor where they were preserved. They
were important documents decidedly, and deserved to be kept
in some safe place of deposit; yet, even this diligent Historian,
with all his painstaking researches, could never get any
glimpse of them. There never were any such returns; and it
is, beyond measure, imprudent at this day to cite such a tale;
but it served its calumnious purpose then, and is reproduced as
fresh as ever to serve the same purpose now.

It would be a pity to dismiss so soon the testimony of the devout Dean; his affidavit continues—

"He might add to these many thousands more; but the diary which he, the deponent, wrote, among the rebels, being burned with his house, books, and all his papers, *he referreth himself to the number in gross*, which the rebels themselves have, upon inquiry, found out and acknowledged, which, notwithstanding, will come short of all that have been murdered in Ireland, there being above one hundred and fifty and four thousand now wanting of the British within the very precinct of Ulster. And the deponent further saith, that it was common table-talk amongst the rebels that the ghosts of Mr William Fullerton, Timothy Jephes, and the most of those who were thrown over Portadown bridge, were daily and nightly seen to walk upon the river, sometimes singing of psalms, sometimes brandishing of naked swords, and sometimes screeching in the most hideous and fearful manner. The deponent did not believe the same at first, and yet is doubtful whether to believe it or not; but saith that divers of the rebels assured him that they themselves did dwell near to the said river, and being daily frighted with these apparitions (but especially with their horrible screeching) were, in conclusion, forced to remove further into the country. Their own priests and friars could not deny the truth thereof; but as oft as it was by deponent objected unto them, they said, that it was but a cunning sleight of the devil to hinder this great work of propagating the Catholic religion, and killing of heretics; or that it was wrought by witchcraft. The deponent himself lived within thirteen miles of the bridge, and never heard any man so much as doubt of the truth thereof; howsoever the deponent obligeth no man's faith, in regard he saw it not with his own eyes; otherwise he had as much certainty as morally could be required of such a matter."

The Dean, you observe, "obligeth no man's faith," except in such cases as the pillar of fire, and the silent Papist dogs and cocks, and the bad boy, whom *he knew.*

Many readers may now begin to be of opinion that they have had enough of Froude's forty folios of abominations; but I must give those readers still another dose of the "eternal witness of blood;"—for let it not be forgotten that these documents form the whole foundation for the superstructure raised by Temple, Borlase, Leland, and Froude, and the whole justification for the policy of England in Ireland during these last two hundred years. The record must not be dismissed too lightly in justice to the First Living Historian. I had thought it was exploded long ago; but now that this illustrious person has taken his stand upon it, and not only rested upon it his own credit as a historian, but also the whole subsequent policy of *his* country in relation to *my* country, there is a real necessity of probing it to the bottom and letting the light through it. Dean Maxwell's discourse—the most fructifying sermon that divine ever preached in his life, for it placed upon his head a bloody mitre, encircled by a black *aureole* of perjury—has now been sufficiently exposed, though far from completely. Nothing would be easier, if the task were not so revolting, than to disgust all decent people with minute narratives of most grotesque obscenity, and cruelty more ingeniously horrible than ever entered into the head of an Iroquois; but the reader must be content with a few samples of the tamer sort. It will be observed that the deponents who swear to the horrid facts were in general mercifully dispensed from the pain of seeing them with their own eyes. Here is a hideous matter which somebody in Kilkenny told Mr William Lucas—"taking a rise" out of William, as Kilkenny fellows are too apt to do:—

"William Lucas, of the city of Kilkenny, deposeth, That although he lived in the town till about five or six weeks past, in which time, he is assured, divers murders and cruel acts were committed, yet he durst not go abroad to see any of them; but he doth confidently believe that the rebels having brought seven Protestants' heads, whereof one was the head of Mr Bingham, a minister, they did then and there, as triumphs of their victories, set them upon the market-cross on a market day; and that the rebels slashed, stabbed, and mangled those heads; put a gag, or carrot, in the said Mr Bingham's mouth, slit up his cheeks to his ears, laying a leaf of a Bible before him, and bid him preach, for his mouth was wide enough; and, after they had solaced themselves, threw those heads into a hole in St James's Green. Jurat. August 16, 1643."

Some of Mr Froude's general statements, as I have before shown, are accurately confirmed by affidavit upon affidavit. If anybody doubts that "the wicked rebels" did really burn women and children in a house, and cut them to pieces if they tried to come out, let that doubter only read what an unknown woman, without a name, did *absolutely* tell the Widow Stanhaw :—

" Christian Stanhaw, the relict of Henry Stanhaw, late of the county of Armagh, esquire, deposeth, That a woman that formerly lived near Laugale, absolutely informed this deponent that the rebels enforced a great number of Protestants, men, women, and children into a house, which they set on fire purposely to burn them, as they did ; and still as any of them offered to come out to shun the fire, the wicked rebels, with scythes, which they had in their hands, cut them to pieces, and cast them into the fire, and burned them with the rest. Jurat.   July 28, 1642."

Poor Mrs Jane Stewart, residing in the town of Sligo, had, on a certain day, the good luck to be confined to her bed by sickness ; and a piece of rare good fortune it was for Jane, seeing she was thus saved from the fate decreed to all the Protestants of that quiet town, and preserved alive to contribute her chapter to the " eternal witness of blood." She deposeth and saith—

" All the men, women, and children of the British that then could be found within the same town (saving this deponent, *who was so sick that she could not stir*) were summoned to go into the gaol, as many as could be met with, all were carried and put into the gaol, where, about twelve o'clock in the night, they were stripped stark naked, and after most of them were cruelly and barbarously murdered with swords, axes, and skeins, and particularly by two butchers, named James Buts and Robert Buts, of Sligo, who murdered many of them ; wherein also were actors, Charles O'Connor, the friar, and Hugh O'Connor aforenamed, brother to the said Teigue O'Connor, Kedagh O'Hart, labourer, Richard Walsh, and Thomas Walsh, the one the jailer the other a butcher, and divers others whom she cannot name, and saith that above thirty of the British which were so put into the gaol, were then and there murdered ; besides Robert Gumble, then Provost of the said town of Sligo, Edward Nusham, and Edward Mercer, who were wounded and left for dead amongst the rest, and Joe Stewart, this deponent's son, which four being the next day found alive, yet all besmeared with blood, were spared to live. All which particulars the deponent was credibly told by those that escaped, and by her Irish servants and others of the town, and further saith, that on the said sixth day of January, there were murdered in the streets of the town of Sligo these British Protestants following, namely, William Shiels and John Shiels, his son, &c., and that they of the Irish that came to bury them stood up to the mid-leg in the blood and brains of those that were so murdered, who were carried out, and cast into a pit digged for that purpose in the garden of Mr Ricrofts, minister of Sligo."

Poor Jane Stewart, lying on her sick-bed, did not see anything of it herself, but I think she had bad dreams.

Why should I wade any more through all this blood and brains? The reader must be weary of it, if not sick. Let it be sufficient to say that folio after folio, with *Jurat, Jurat* upon the pages, is full charged and reeking with the same kind of abomination. By far the greater part of the depositions are sworn upon hearsay, yet now and then a man comes boldly up and swears that he saw dreadful things with his own eyes. For example:—

" James Geare, of the county of Monaghan, deposeth, That the rebels at Clownes murdered one James Netterville, proctor to the minister there, who, although he was diversely wounded, his belly ripped up, and his entrails taken out, and laid above a yard from him, yet he bled not at all until they lifted him up, and carried him away, at which this deponent being an eye-witness, much wondered; and thus barbarously they used him, after they had drawn him to go to Mass with them."

Another saw an " Irish rebel " make three passes with his drawn sword point-blank into the body of a woman, she with hands clasped defying him to hurt her unless God permitted him, and accordingly the sword never grazed her skin, and the wicked rebel walked off much discomfited, and all the on-lookers mightily marvelled. Yet another swearer tells how the " rebels " took a Scotchman (they seldom have any names, neither the rebels nor victims), and having cut open his body to get at his "small guts," they did nail the end of said small guts to a tree, and then whipped the Scotchman round and round the tree, until all that intestine was drawn out and wound neatly round the trunk, then whipped him back again till it was unwound, and all this, as they said, to find out whether a Scotchman's gut or a dog's is the longer.

We have seen that the Historian scarcely names one of the swearers, except Dean Maxwell, whose testimony is the rock and strong tower to our Protestant interest; that he never gives any of the words of the swearers, and carefully omits any allusion to ghosts and miracles; but in one instance he has actually named another witness, Adam Clover, of the county Cavan, and gives him as authority for an act of cruelty perpetrated by three Irishwomen, who stripped a Protestant woman naked at the time of her child-birth, and left her and her child to die. I am delighted to find that he knows Adam Clover; but why not give us a little more of what Adam saw with his own eyes—for Adam was a good swearer. Why does our Historian withhold from his admiring readers such a choice horror as that which follows. Now Adam Clover deposeth and saith—

"That he *observed* thirty persons to be barbarously murdered, and about 150 more cruelly wounded, so that traces of blood, issuing from them, lay upon the high road for twelve miles together; and many very young children were left and perished by the way, to the number of sixty or thereabouts."

Mr Froude's friend Adam does not say where he *observed* all this, nor on what road, nor between what towns, nor by whom, nor upon whom the murders and other cruelties were committed. At any rate we see here an example of the manner in which this great Historian manipulates his authorities, presenting only those particulars which he thinks may go down, with credulous people, and suppressing the rest.

One blunder, however, he has made, in calling attention at all to the atrocious cruelties charged in these oaths against Irishmen and Irishwomen, as perpetrated upon helpless women and children of another nationality. At no time in their history have the Irish—our proud, fierce, generous Irish—been capable of cruelty to women and children, no, nor to the defenceless men. If Froude wants to tell of massacres, let him consult the annals of his own country; let him go back to St Brice's day, 1002, at cockcrow in the morning, and feed full on horrors; or let him tell how the same Saxon slaves, who massacred their Danish masters on St Brice's day, afterwards formed a plot to massacre their French masters in the time of William the Conqueror; or let him turn his eyes a moment to the wild valley of Glencoe, and tell how King William's Protestant soldiers knew how to deal with women and infants.

Mr Froude is right in saying that England and Ireland will never arrive at a good understanding until the business of the "massacre" (that turning point in history) shall have been fully cleared up. It is true, but *he* has not cleared it up; nor was that his intention. The man's idea has been that the public would take his very general account of the matter, and rest upon his authority for those *other* authorities which ought to support him. He never was more mistaken in his life; and I shall be much deceived if the examination of that portion of Irish history, an examination which is now sure to go on, does not end in the gibbeting of Froude on high, as the most immoral of historic impostors.

My next chapter will finish his delinquencies as to the " massacres," and I shall afterwards have to show that, in compiling the history subsequent to that, he has proved himself even more recklessly and desperately depraved.

CHAPTER V.

TOO MUCH FROUDE.

SOME readers, by this time, may be disposed to say, we have
enough of Froude; he is already a notoriously convicted
impostor, and no historian; and it is making too much of him
to keep pursuing him in this way.   Certainly, it is making too
much of *Froude* himself, whose literary pretensions I estimate
very low, and whose historic merits are far less than nothing.
He composes fiction in a picturesque style; and ought to have
confined himself to that species of composition.   He could
match Mrs Emma Southworth, or our graphic fellow-country-
man, Captain Mayne Reid.   If he would contribute a striking
tale of horror to the New-York *Weekly Fee-Faw*, he could
command more per column than ever did Sylvanus Cobb; but
he had no call to the writing of history.   However, it still
seems needful to expose a little more of his "misdealing," as
Prendergast mildly terms it, in the matter of the great
"Massacre" of 1641.

" You, who would form an independent opinion on the
matter, I would advise to read (*whatever else you read*) Sir
John Temple's History of the Rebellion, and Dr Borlase's
History of it.   Temple was, as I said; an eye-witness.
Borlase's book contains, in the appendix, large selections from
the evidence taken on oath before the Commissioners at
Dublin."

This is from the impostor's last lecture, in reply to Father
Burke.   His main authority for the whole story is still Temple;
for Borlase is but a reproduction of Temple's History, and
they are both founded wholly upon the famous Depositions.
In this passage, then, as well as in his new book, Froude
commits himself and his readers entirely to the testimony of

the eloquent Master of the Rolls; and he does not whisper one hint of the fact, that Sir John Temple himself, a few years later, tried to suppress that book. Froude knows, of course, (for what is there that he does not know?)—but thinks his readers may not have met with the published "Letters of his Excellency Arthur Capel, Earl of Essex, Lord-Lieutenant of Ireland." It is no abstruse State-paper pigeon-hole I refer him to; the book was printed in London, 1770, a fair quarto; and it stands upon the shelves of all historic libraries; and we learn from it, that in the year 1674 Lord Essex was soliciting from the English Government a considerable grant for Temple —five hundred pounds a year, "on the forfeited estates." And the Ministry seems to have made the republication of Temple's History an objection against the grant, which objection Lord Essex, on the part of his friend, thus endeavours to remove—

EXTRACT OF A LETTER FROM THE EARL OF ESSEX, LORD-LIEUTENANT OF IRELAND, TO MR SECRETARY COVENTRY:—

"I am to acknowledge the receipt of yours of the 22nd of December, wherein you mention a book that was newly published, concerning the cruelties committed in Ireland, at the beginning of the late war. Upon further inquiry, I find Sir J. Temple, Master of the Rolls here, author of that book, was this last year sent to by several stationers of London, to have his consent to the printing thereof. But he assures me that he utterly denies it; and whoever printed it, did it without his knowledge. Thus much I thought fit to add to what I formerly said upon this occasion, that I might do this gentleman right, in case it was suspected he had any share in publishing this new edition."

"He utterly *denied* it;" that is, did not absolutely deny that he had written and published the book, but only denied that he had given permission to any stationers to reprint the offensive thing; and his friend Lord Essex pleads this in order "to do the gentleman right." In fact the grant of an annuity was made; poor Sir John Temple never had enough. He was already an "Adventurer" under the Parliamentary arrangement for dividing the confiscated lands; he had in-

D

vested money in the "Massacre," and I find his name amongst the subscribers to the fund of the "gentlemen adventurers," but he always wanted *more, more*, being the son of a horse-leech's daughter, and he got more and more. Now, some innocent reader, greener than the rest, will say, well, at least the poor man was ashamed at last of his naughty book, and endeavoured to make people forget it. Alas! no, he was not ashamed; but the *Restoration* had occurred in the meantime; the Stuarts had come back; Charles II. was King; about the Court there was supposed to be much Papistry, and a hard-working Protestant feared that his former zealous labours in doing "the work of the Lord" might not meet with such recognition and encouragement as they were assured of under the godly government of the Lord Protector.

But Temple's abandonment and repudiation of his nasty work does not suit Froude at all. Froude has no idea of permitting a man who has laid such a fine cockatrice egg to fling it aside to rot; no, he (Froude) will pick up that egg, warm it, *sit on* it, hoping to hatch it into a venomous brood. It is true the egg is long ago rotten, and even we, Protestants, have noses, which we much hold when things grow too fœtid.

So much for Temple. "Read Temple," says Froude, "whatever else you read, you who would form an independent opinion."

The Doctor is, perhaps, next after Temple, the favourite authority relied upon by our Impostor-Historian; although, in citing the Doctor at all, Froude feels that he is making a too great concession to Irish susceptibilities. From Temple's account of 154,000 Protestants, whose throats were cut in Ulster alone, the Doctor, in his estimate, subtracts 116,000, and Petty is mentioned by Froude as an authority not likely to be unfavourable to the Irish; so much he claims for him in one of his lectures, and in his book he terms that clever Doctor "a cool-headed, sceptical sort of man," whose computation is surely not excessive! Cool-headed! well, this is true; a cooler head, or a cooler hand, did not appear in those days within the four seas of Ireland than Doctor Petty. The value of him, as an "authority," might, perhaps, be questioned, for at the time of the alleged "massacre" he was a boy; had never been in Ireland at all; was at that time learning his trade, that of a carpenter, in the city of Caen, in France, and it was only in the track of Cromwell's army that he took up his empty carpet-bag, and went to make his fortune in Ireland. A biographical sketch of this extraordinary person was written and published about six months ago—before there was any word of Froude's Lectures or History—by a citizen of Brooklyn—not Mr Meline, but another citizen, whose name is Major Muskerry—from which sketch I may venture to give an extract or two altogether appropriate in this place, and let the reader be assured that the career of Doctor Sir William is worth some study, as that of the most successful land-pirate—for a private adventurer—and most voracious land-shark who ever appeared in Western Europe. The Doctor is authority for most of his story himself; but here we cite the words of Major Muskerry:—

"Quitting Caen in 1643, when he was twenty years old, he spent a little time in England, and then, as the war had checked the industries of the country, he voyaged again and spent three years in France and the Netherlands. Here he studied medicine, and helped his younger brother, Anthony, in his schooling, their father being now dead. He was not fond of explaining how he managed to get along during these years. But he mentions that when he returned to England with his brother, he had saved seventy pounds beyond his expenses. He must have carried on some kind of peddlery, or perhaps acted as agent in the sale of English cloth. He was a man of shifts, and must have had severe experiences, for he told his friend Aubrey that he once lived for a week in Paris on twopence worth of walnuts—"bread at discretion" being beyond his means. Aubrey used to say he suspected Petty had been put into a French prison for something. And it is very likely the young trafficker ran into somebody's debt, and so lost his liberty for a time, in the good old feudal fashion.

"While he was in Paris, Petty became acquainted with Hobbes, the philosopher, and studied the 'Anatomy of Vesalius' along with him, at the same time drawing the diagrams of a treatise on optics, which that old 'Leviathan' was then writing. In 1646, Petty returned to England. He then carried his French learning to Oxford, where it was recognized; and in three years he got his degree of M.D. at that

College. He was also admitted into the London College of Physicians."

There was nothing that Petty could not learn, if there was money in it; and he spent some years as a projector and an inventor; but without distinguished success, until, in a happy hour, he bethought him of the mighty spoils in Ireland, which the massacre had placed within the reach of every God-fearing Englishman who would invest a little money in it, and "seek the Lord" with his whole heart. Here follows some more from his Brooklyn biographer—

"But there was another great field of effort and enterprise now opened before the eyes of Dr Petty—the field of Ireland. Cromwell had beaten down the Irish Confederation, and the English Parliament was arranging the plan of driving the native Irish out of three provinces of Ireland into Connaught. Ten thousand English adventurers seized their carpet-bags, and swarmed into the confiscated island. Among these was Dr Petty, one of the ablest brains ever exercised over the area of a conquered country. He got himself appointed at once to an Irish office of high character—that of Physician to the Army in Ireland. He landed at Waterford in September, 1652. He himself records that he was worth about £500 when he came to Ireland. His biography is composed in a great measure from notices left by himself, and he repeatedly mentions the sums in his possession at the several crises of his life, as if they were the chief points of interest. But the most remarkable part of the business is that these notices occur in his will written at the end of his life. He mixes biography and bequests together, as if he meant to save space and time, and show himself an economist to the last. It is certainly one of the most singular wills on record, exhibiting some of the most enlightened ideas of social polity, jumbled with the penurious apologies of a genuine mammon-scraper familiar with much of the sharp practice of his time. But his intimations are very brief, and the story of his acquisitions was one he would not care to tell at any length, very probably. He slurs things over, like Richard Boyle, first Earl of Cork.

"He tells enough, however, to show that this gathering of Irish property were large and rapid. He says he was appointed to survey the Irish estates, and in this way made

£9000, which sum, with other smaller items, including salaries
as Doctor and as Clerk of the Council of Dublin, enabled him
to purchase land at a time 'when men bought as much land
for ten shillings as in 1685 yielded the same amount per
annum.' Aubrey says his lands brought in a rental of £18,000;
which would be about £40,000, and over, at the present day,
say 200,000 dols."

The Doctor was returned to Parliament (Richard Cromwell's
Parliament) in 1658. A certain Jerome Sankey was a member
of the same Parliament, who was a large "adventurer" in
Ireland upon the confiscated estates, as well as Petty, but who
had been overreached by the smart Doctor and his "Ring" in
the matter of land-grabbing. This is not wonderful; the
Doctor as Surveyor had many chances; and as he was relied
upon for "setting out" lands for whole regiments and brigades,
he had endless opportunities of buying up for little or nothing
estates of great value. The Doctor had surveys made, and all
the fieldwork done by private soldiers instructed by himself;
"hardy men," says Prendergast, "fittest to ruffle with the
rude spirits they were like to encounter, who might not see
without a grudge their ancient inheritance, the only support of
their wives and children, measured out before their eyes for
strangers to occupy; and they must often, when at work, be
in danger of a surprise from Tories." In fact, many of them
were surprised and captured, and lost their ears, as tithe-
proctors and bailiffs did in late years; but, on the whole,
Doctor Sir William and his friends had not only the large discretion which the survey gave them, but could, very often,
when some Cromwellian officer or soldier came to see his lot,
gravely show him a few leagues of quaking black bog, and the
poor fellow instantly offered to sell his estate for a horse to
ride away upon; so that the county Meath tradition about the
"White Horse of the Peppers" was not only true in fact, but
was only a sample of many bargains in landed estate which
took place in those days, under the prudent administration of
the Doctor. In short, he had so many advantages over his
brethren of the carpet-bag, that Sir Jerome Sankey could
stand it no longer. Especially there was the case of some very
fine lands, the Liberties of Limerick. One Capt. Winkworth,
a prayerful officer of the Protector's army, had obtained an

order for this coveted district; at least the Captain thought his order covered that place, and so he presented his credentials to the Doctor, as Surveyor-General, who told him those lands were "reserved." This forms one of the many charges brought by Sir Jerome against the Doctor in his speech in Parliament. "Why, then, Mr Speaker (said Sir Jerome) there's Captain Winkworth; Captain Winkworth came with an order for the Liberties of Limerick; but *the Doctor said:* 'Captain, will you sell? Will you sell?' 'No,' said the Captain, 'it is the price of my blood.' Then said the Doctor, "'Tis bravely said. Why, then, my noble Captain, the Liberties of Limerick are meat for your master, meaning the Lord Deputy,'" and so forth. In short, the Doctor was bound to give the best things within his own "Ring." But Petty says that Sankey's real cause of quarrel with him was that he, Petty, "had stopped Sankey's unrighteous order for rejecting 3000 acres fallen to him by lot, and enabling him arbitrarily to elect the same quantity in its stead, thus rejecting at his pleasure what God had predetermined for his lot." The Doctor retorted upon Sir Jerome with much bad language, for he had a rough and rasping tongue, and the other carpet-bagger challenged him. Petty accepted, and being the challenged party, and having choice of weapons, and being somewhat short-sighted, but a skilful carpenter, he chose *adzes*, in a dark cellar; this proposal was thought too professional by the "friends" of the other carpet-bagger. It was as if you quarrelled with the first mate of a whaling-ship, and challenged him, and he selected for weapons *harpoons*, stipulating that the duel should be fought from two boats in the open sea. The duel never in fact took place. But such a storm of inquiry was raised, that Sir Richard Cromwell, the Lord-Lieutenant, could not protect his physician, and the latter was dismissed from his public employments.

I resume the narrative of Major Muskerry, citizen of Brooklyn No. 2 :—

"Then came the flurry of 1660, when Charles II. came back again. Petty did not grieve much for the Cromwells. He went to see his Majesty soon after his arrival at White-hall, and his Majesty 'was mightily pleased with his discourse'—the discourse of a richer man than himself. Petty could lend the King money, and perhaps he did. At any rate, that menace of Parliamentary "inquiry" went off with the Roundheads, and in 1662 Petty was made one of a Court of Commissioners for Irish Estates, and Surveyor-General of Ireland. He was also knighted, and on his arrival in Ireland, was returned to the Irish Parliament for Enniscorthy. Still he did not escape entirely scot-free. The 'Court of Innocents,' which sat in the Irish capital, found that he had got much ground that belonged to 'innocent Papists,' and so he disgorged some of his acquisitions—'great part,' he says himself. But he still retained an enormous property. From one hill in Kerry it was said he could look round and see no ground that did not belong to himself. That was the hill of Maugerto, now spelled Mangerton—the rude old peak of the Devil's Punch Bowl, on which, perhaps, some of my readers have stood and looked down on the Lake of Killarney.

" Sir William Petty goes on to explain the swift rise of his fortunes. He says he lived within his income, set up iron works and pilchard fishing, opened lead mines and old timber. But of course he did not tell everything, nor mention half the advantages which his position brought to his hands. His fortunes grew from the ruins of a thousand old Irish families ejected from the county of Kerry, and time has only quadrupled the value of the territory he won for his descendants."

I need not follow the fortunes of that smart Doctor any further. Enough to say that, when he grew rich, he bribed one of the poor high-born but beggared Geraldine Fitzmaurices to marry his daughter, and also to take his paltry name of Petty. The great estate afterwards came to the present Lansdownes, whose surname is Petty-Fitzmaurice, at the reader's service. This last affair is a matter of no consequence ; the thing that I specially note here is that Doctor Sir William Petty, the man in all Ireland who had most money invested in the " massacre," who made most profit on his investment, who had the largest interest in establishing the grand fact of the " massacre "—that this land-pirate is palmed off upon us by the impostor, Froude, as a witness for the said grand fact ; nay, as the most moderate witness and most favourable to the Irish people. He cannot see more in it—this moderate and friendly Sir William—than (say) 38,000 throats cut in the massacre ; a pretty fair and handsome massacre, a, valid and substantial massacre for history to make a turning-point of, and for the Lansdowne estates to derive title from.

Indeed, our bold Doctor was the great administrator of the whole Transplantation ; he *ran* the Transplantation, and he ran the massacre into the ground, but in the most pious and God-fearing spirit. His own candid autobiographical notes let us perceive, that for himself he believed neither in a God nor in anything else, except in the value of acres of ground ; yet when he had contracted with the Government and the army to make an accurate survey and maps of the confiscated lands, he did not dare to begin this mighty work for the glory of God without—but here I call in the aid of Prendergast—

"This great step in perfecting the scheme of plantation was consecrated with all the forms of religion, the articles being signed by Doctor Petty in the Council Chamber of Dublin Castle, on the 11th of December, 1654, in the presence of many of the chief officers of the army, after a solemn seeking of God performed by Colonel Thomlinson, for a blessing upon the conclusion of so great a business."

It will be remembered that in the first chapter I cited from Froude, that passage in which he says that the Irish were endowed by Providence with a lovely land ; but that " they had pared its forests to the stump, and left it shivering in dampness and desolation ;" and I requested the reader to bear that in mind.   Now, the chief parer of the forests was Froude's friend, Doctor Sir William. He knew the use of an axe right well ; and if he was disappointed in his wish to hew down Sir Jerome Sankey in the cellar, he could, at least, fell oaks and beeches in Kerry. Students of Irish history know, that the Irish were never very solicitous to clear away their fine forests ; and that it was the English commanders in Elizabeth's reign who made the first serious inroads upon those waving woods, when they had occasion to open up passes into the Irish enemy's "fastnesses."   Froude knows particularly well that the successive occupiers of "forfeited estates," who were always sensible, in those days, of the precariousness of their tenure, always aware that a new settlement, unsettlement, resettlement, a new " resumption," confiscation, revolution, or general bedevilment of all things, might come upon them any day, thought they could do no better than realise the value, at least, of the woods while they had them. ' To get a crop of wheat a man must plough and sow, and wait for the season; but he can cut down and sell a tree at any time, or a-hundred thousand trees. The reason why I say "Froude knows" all this, is that the whole process is very clearly set forth in the "Report of the Commissioners appointed by the Parliament of England to take cognizance of the properties that were confiscated upon the Irish who were concerned in the Rebellion of 1688, &c." Froude knows this Report, because it is not abstruse nor recondite; and if it were abstruse or recondite he would then know it still better; for he admits that he knows everything. The Commissioners, in section 77 of their Report, say, that "dreadful havoc had been committed upon the woods of the proscribed;" and they further say, "Those upon whom the confiscated lands have been bestowed, or their agents, have been so greedy to seize upon the most trifling profits that large trees have been cut down and sold for sixpence each." They say also, "this destruction is still carried on in many parts of the country." And so it continued to be carried on, not by the Irish, but by holders of forfeited estates, until Dean Swift, some years later, lamented that in the once well-wooded island there was not left timber enough for housebuilding or for shipbuilding, and that the land had a naked and dreary appearance for want of trees. Now, it was bad enough in these rascals to pare our forests to the stump; but this British historical being, coming forward at the present day to complain to the civilized world that *we*, the Irish, pared our forests to the stump, might be thought to add insult to injury; and if he means so, it is his mission.

It is in the county of Kerry chiefly that the Parliamentary Commissioners specify the cruel havoc made in Irish woods; and it was in the county of Kerry that Dr Sir William Petty had his principal estates. For years the vales of Dunkerron and Iveragh rung with the continual fall of giant oaks. There was a good market; Spain and France were searching the world for pipe-staves; in English dockyards there was steady demand for shipknees; and Sir William knew exactly where there was the best market for everything. In Ireland itself,

also, he set on foot ironworks, and fed the fires from his own
woods; that is, woods which were not his own, and from
which the right owners might expel him some day.   There
was no source of profit, known to the commerce and traffic of
that day, in which Sir William did not bear a hand; he "took
hold" of everything that was available and saleable, after first
" seeking the Lord" in the midst of his " Ring" of Saints; for
Sir William was truly one of the elect.   When he went to his
" Down survey," along with some faithful officers of the Army
of the Saints, I find an affecting narrative of a truly touching
scene, Doctor Sir William and his swaddling " Ring" upon
their marrow-bones, wrestling with the Lord, with strong
crying and tears, calling upon the Lord (stand and deliver !) to
bless the great work.   Bravo ! Doctor Sir William, go forward
boldly, and seize and divide this mighty spoil.   You never had
such a chance in all your varied life before; there were no such
prizes in the carpenters' shops of Caen; profits upon pills in
London suburbs were nothing in comparison with the victorious
sharing of these wide vales of Munster.   Yea, the gleaming of
the grapes of Ephraim is better than the clusters of Manasseh.
Go ahead, then, prosperously, and ride victorious, Oh ! Doctor;
for behold the earth and the fulness thereof is thine ; and thy
name shall be called, not Petty, but Mahershall-hash-baz, " for
he hasteth unto the dividing of the spoil."

CHAPTER VI.

EVIDENCE OF THE MASSACRE OF 1641.

THE reader can now estimate the value of the evidence for the "Massacre" of 1641. The Reverend Ferdinando Warner, a Protestant clergyman, gives this account of the matter :—

"It is easy enough to demonstrate the falsehood of the relation of every Protestant historian of this rebellion."

It would be hard, indeed, upon us Protestants, if we were compelled to support and maintain those raw-head-and-bloody-bones histories; but fortunately there is no such compulsion upon us. Mr Warner was not one of the "gentlemen adventurers;" he expected no lands, nor money, out of the "Massacre;" he wrote his history with the single desire to report the truth; and although he had a horror of the "rebellion," and of Popery and priests, we see that he felt himself free to denounce the gory falsehood. It is true that his researches did lead him to conclude that there were murders of Protestants within the three or four months, to the number of two thousand and upward; but this estimate is liable to be more than questioned. In fact, all writers on the subject, including even Temple and Froude, agree that the slaughter of those Protestant colonists did not enter into the plan of the insurrection at all, the sole object being to drive away the intruders and resume possession of the lands so lately confiscated. Sir John Temple himself says :—

"It was resolved *not to kill any*, but where of necessity they should be forced thereunto by opposition."

And Warner says :—

"Their first intention went no farther than to strip the English and the Protestants of their power and possessions; and, unless forced to it by opposition, *not to shed any blood.*"

"Resistance," (says Leland,) "produced some bloodshed; and, in some instances, private revenge, religious hatred, and the suspicion of some valuable concealment, enraged the triumphant rebels to insolence, cruelty, and murder. So far, however, was the *original scheme* of the conspiracy at first pursued, that *few fell by the sword, except in open war and assault.*"

A volume was published by another Protestant clergyman, and a contemporary of the event; which Froude notices in this cavalier style :—

" At that time there was a Protestant parson in Ireland, who called himself a Minister of the Word of God. He gives his account of the whole transaction in a letter to the people of England, begging of them to help their fellow-Protestants of Ireland. Here are his words :—

" ' It was the intention of the Irish to massacre all the English. On Saturday they were to disarm them, on Sunday to seize all their cattle and goods, and on Monday they were to cut all the English throats. The former they executed ; the third—that is the massacre—they failed in.' "

It would surely be a curious circumstance that they " failed in " the massacre, if massacre had been their intention, seeing that the Ulster Protestants were entirely at their mercy. But the Historian cannot endure Protestants, like Mr Warner and this other " parson," who cast a doubt over the grand fact. A pretty " Protestant," indeed ! who tries to make the " turning-point " in history turn the wrong way ! A horrible, cool-blooded massacre there was, there must have been, or else our Protestant interest is surrendered ; so the Historian still stands upon his thirty-eight thousand mangled corpses. Yet he tries to uphold the story by some other evidence than that of the adventurers who had money in it. So he gives us, in a note, a passage from Richard Beling's *Vindiciæ Catholicorum Hiberniæ.* Beling was a Catholic ; and the fraudulent Historian tells us that he " half confirms, in shame, Sir Phelim O'Neill's barbarities." He gives the passage in Beling's Latin, and it states that O'Neill, for the sake of revenge (or retaliation) did raise tumults and enact tragic scenes in some parts of Ulster, which are the less to be commended—*if the stories are true*—on the part of a man who is a Catholic. If the stories are true, we would all say that, and without " half confirming " the truth of them. If Sir Phelim, or his people did really slaughter defenceless people, with their women and infants, unless it were in retaliation for the like outrages committed by the other side, every one would admit that such conduct cannot be commended, if, as Beling says, "*si vera referuntur.*" In short, the Historian of the turning-point fails entirely to produce evidence of any massacre at all, except the evidence of men notoriously living by the said massacre.

But there was *retaliation*, in the course of the war. Certainly, when the sword is once drawn, retaliation *in kind* for outrage committed contrary to the laws of war is not only a right but a duty. It would have been cruelty on the part of Sir Phelim and the other Irish leaders, cruelty towards their own people, if he had failed in such a case to repay slaughter with slaughter. Even this was done with great moderation, and to a trifling extent; nor is there to be found, I think, in history, another example of an insurrection, by an oppressed and despoiled people, commenced and carried on so bloodlessly for at least two months. Here, then, it becomes of vital interest to the truth of history to ascertain which side began the murdering calling for retaliation. And this carries us at once to Island Magee.

Irish writers, as well as the constant tradition of the country, have represented the slaughter of the peaceful, unarmed people of Island Magee by the Scotch garrison of Carrickfergus as the first unprovoked act of butchery. Island Magee is a peninsula, six miles long, by one and a half in breadth, attached to the coast of Antrim, and running northward parallel to that coast, from the entrance to Carrickfergus Bay. It is a very fertile district, and has always been thickly peopled. In November, 1641, it held not only its own permanent inhabitants, but also some hundreds more who had betaken themselves to that remote place, to live for a time with their kindred, and avoid the troubles of the time.

The peninsula rises gradually from west to east, and its eastern side sinks down perpendicularly to the sea in a wall of cliff, four hundred feet high. On one fatal night, when the people were all in their beds, a force of Munroe's soldiers, from the garrison of Carrickfergus, issued forth in silence, and traversed the whole peninsula, gathering the people as they went, and goading them forward, unarmed men and half-naked women, with children in their arms or at their knees; and so drove them to the brink of the steep, where a pebble dislodged from the edge will fall into deep water; and then, Hurrah for the Protestant Interest! One volley and a bayonet charge or two, and the shrieking multitude was forced *over*. They were all dead before they reached the water. Ferguson, himself, an Antrim Protestant, tells the tale in some verses, describing the escape of a man and woman to Scotland in an open boat, upon that same night:

> The midnight moon is wading deep;
>   The land sends off the gale;
> The boat beneath the sheltering steep;
>   Hangs on a seaward sail;
> And, leaning o'er the weather-rail,
>   The lovers hand in hand,
> Take their last look of Innisfail;
>   " Farewell, doomed Ireland !
>
> " And art thou doomed to discord still ?
>   And shall thy sons ne'er cease
> To search and struggle for thine ill ?
>   Ne'er share thy good in peace ?
> Already do thy mountains feel
>   Avenging Heaven's ire ?
> Hark—hark—this is no thunder peal,
>   That was no lightning fire ! "
>
> It was no fire from heaven he saw,
>   For, far from hill and dell,
> O'er Gobbin's brow the mountain flaw
>   Bears musket-shot, and yell,
> And shouts of brutal glee, that tell
>   A foul and fearful tale,
> While over blast and breaker swell
>   Thin shrieks and woman's wail.
>
> Now fill they far the upper sky,
>   Now down 'mid air they go,
> The frantic scream, the piteous cry,
>   The groan of rage and woe;
> And wilder in their agony
>   And shriller still they grow—
> Now cease they, choking suddenly;
>   The waves boom on below.

This is the massacre of Island Magee, and the first real butchery of the war, as the Irish have always steadily insisted,

Whether it befel in November, 1641, or in the ensuing January; whether three thousand people were there murdered, as Irish authorities allege, or only "thirty families," as Dr Leland declares, or thirty persons, as Mr Froude tells us upon his own authority; on all these points there is a controversy, and, no doubt, will continue to be. Froude, following Leland, places the incident in January, that it may appear to be an act of retaliation for other outrages which, he says, the Irish had been guilty of on their side. Now, Dr Leland is no authority at all, because he was not yet born a hundred years after. But our Historian quite complacently cites the authority of a Dr Reid, author of a History of the Irish Presbyterians, and who cannot allow that his Scotch clients tumbled over the cliff more than "thirty persons," counting only the heads of Leland's thirty families. "Every detail of that business," says Froude, "has been preserved, and can be traced to the minutest fibre of it:" and in a note, "The particulars are given exactly by Dr Reid." Now, I know this decent clergyman, a country minister dwelling in the village of Rathmelton, Donegal county,—if he still lives. If he were to narrate to me a fact which he saw with his own eyes, I should believe him; but who will accept him as authority for what happened about a hundred and fifty years before he was born? If he said he had dreamed it, or that "the spirits" told him, I should suspect his reverence of being crazy; if he cited anything from the folios of the swearers, I should more than suspect his good faith. And is it not too audacious in Froude to pretend to stop the mouth of all authority and all tradition, with his Doctor of Donegal?

There is no compiler of Irish history more perfectly trustworthy than Dr John Curry; and he has devoted a considerable space to an investigation of the affair of Island Magee. I cannot hope to improve upon his remarks, nor effectively to condense them. He says:—

"The report that his Majesty's Protestant subjects first fell upon, and murdered the Roman Catholics, got credit and reputation, and was openly and frequently asserted," says Jones, Bishop of Meath, in a letter to Dr Borlase, 1679. And Sir Audley Mervin, Speaker of the House of Commons, in a public speech to the Duke of Ormonde, in 1662, confesses, 'that

several pamphlets then swarmed to fasten the rise of this
rebellion upon the Protestants; and that they drew the first
blood.' And, indeed, whatever cruelties may be charged upon
the Irish in the prosecution of this war, 'their first intention,
we see,' says another Protestant voucher, 'went no further
than to strip the English and the Protestants of their power
and possessions, and, unless forced to it by opposition, not
shed any blood.' Even Temple confesses the same; for,
mentioning what mischiefs were done in the beginning of this
insurrection, 'certainly,' says he, 'that which these rebels
mainly intended at first, and most busily employed themselves
about, was the driving away the Englishmen's cattle, and
possessing themselves of their goods.'

"In a MS. journal of an officer in the King's service,
quoted by Mr Carte, wherein there is a minute and daily
account of everything that happened in the North of Ireland,
during the first weeks of the insurrection, there is not even an
insinuation of any cruelties committed by the insurgents on the
English or Protestants; although it is computed by the
journalists, 'that the Protestants of that Province had killed
near a thousand of the rebels in the first week or two of the
rebellion.' And on the 16th of November, 1641, 'Mr Robert
Wallbank came from the North, and informed the Irish House
of Commons, that two hundred of the people of Coleraine
fought with one thousand of the rebels, slew six of them, and
not one of themselves hurt. That in another battle, sixty of
the rebels were slain, and only two of the others hurt, none
slain.' Nor do we find, in this account, the least mention of
cruelties then committed by the Irish; but much of the success
and victory of his Majesty's Protestant subjects, as often as they
encountered them.

"It is worthy of particular notice, that a Commission of the
Lords Justices, Parsons and Borlase, dated so late as December 23rd, 1641, was sent down to several gentlemen in Ulster
(where it is agreed on all hands that these cruelties and outrages were chiefly committed), in virtue of which Commission
Temple and Borlase confess 'several examinations were afterwards taken of murders committed by the rebels, and the per-
petrators of many of these murders were discovered. Yet the
Commission itself, though it authorizes these gentlemen 'to

call upon all those who had then suffered in the rebellion, and all the witnesses of these sufferings, to give in examinations of the nature of them, and of every minute circumstance relating to them, expressly and particularly specifying every other crime usual in insurrections, and, then committed, in this, viz.; plunder, robbery, and even traitorous words, actions, and speeches; yet, I say, there is not a syllable mentioned of any murders, then committed, in this Commission, nor any express power given by it to make inquiry into them. From whence it seems necessarily to follow, either that few or no such cruelties had been committed by the insurgents before the 23rd of December, 1641, or that these Lords Justices deemed murders and massacres less worthy of their notice, of being strictly inquired after, than even traitorous words and speeches.

"That a great number of unoffending Irish were massacred in Island Magee, by Scottish Puritans, about the beginning of this insurrection, is not denied by any adverse writer that I have met with. An apology, however, is made for it by them all, which, even if it were grounded on fact, as I shall presently show it is not, would be a very bad one, and seems at least to imply a confession of the charge. These writers pretend that this massacre was perpetrated on those harmless people in revenge of some cruelties before committed by the rebels on the Scots in other parts of Ulster. But as I find this controversy has been already taken up by two able Protestant historians, who seem to differ about the time in which that dismal event happened, perhaps, by laying before the readers the accounts of both, with such animadversions as naturally arise from them, that time may be more clearly and positively ascertained.

"A late learned and ingenious author of a history of Ireland, has shifted off this shocking incident from November, 1641 (in which month it has been generally placed), to January following, many weeks after horrible cruelties (as he tells us) had been committed by the insurgents on the Scots in the North. 'The Scottish soldiers,' says he, 'who had reinforced the garrison of Carrickfergus, were possessed of an habitual hatred of Popery, and inflamed to an implacable detestation of the Irish, by multiplied accounts of their cruelties. In one fatal night, they issued from Carrickfergus, into an adjacent·

E

district called Island Magee, where a number of the poorer
Irish resided, unoffending and untainted with the rebellion.
If we may believe one of the leaders *of this party*, thirty
families were assailed by them in their beds, and massacred
with calm and deliberate cruelty. 'As if,' proceeds the Historian, 'the incident were not sufficiently hideous, Popish
writers have represented it with shocking aggravations."

An angry man was Sir Phelim O'Neill when he heard of
the drowning at Island Magee; but his duty to his own people
called for stern retaliation; and that some acts of this nature
were done, cannot and need not be denied. Sir Phelim was
not naturally disposed to cruelty, and had anxiously sought to
keep his men—wild as they were with their wrongs and
sufferings—within the limits prescribed at the beginning.
Yet he had to give way to some extent; and it must be true
that some Protestants were flung into the Bann river at Portadown, just as Catholics had been flung over the Gobbins cliffs.

I am bound to maintain, after all the examination I have
been able to give to the ghastly story, that the Irish insurrection of 1641 was notable amongst insurrections for its mildness
and humanity; and that, if the Irish were not the most gentle,
patient, and good-natured people in the whole world, their
island would long since have been a smoking wilderness of
cinders soaked in blood.

Sir William Petty, looking calmly into the whole business,
shortly after, says, with his usual coolness, that, at any rate,
" Upon the playing of this game, or match, the English won,
and had, amongst other pretences, a gamester's right at least
to their estates. As for the blood shed in the contest for
these lands, God best knows who did occasion it!" Ah! yes;
God knows; and Petty knew; but could not afford to tell; for
the title to those confiscated estates was at stake; not legally,
indeed, but morally, in the estimation of civilized mankind;
and the prosperous Doctor, having a gloriously winning hand
in that " match or game," was content to enjoy his good luck,
and leave the rest to God. The English did, indeed, win the
game, after ten years of painful struggle and carnage; for
Ireland did not sink under one blow, as Scotland did, at
Dunbar; and this philosophic Doctor was the principal carver
at the mighty feast of spoil. The insurrection was followed

by a general war throughout the island, a war which the Lords of the Council took care to *make* general, because then the confiscations would be general also.

In the course of the war there were some bright days for Ireland, and especially the day of Benburb, for the same covenanting rascal, Munroe, who slew the poor people of Island Magee, had the ill-luck, six years later, on a bright June day, to look in the face of the greatest of all the O'Neills, the magnificent Owen Roe. It is one of the shining points in our history, gleaming through the general darkness, on whose brightness Irish eyes love to dwell. Therefore, in this large History of Ireland, Mr Froude takes care never to mention how, on that bright summer day, General Munroe marched along the northern bank of the Blackwater with a formidable army, making no doubt that he would dislodge and disperse the Irish chiefs and their clansmen. But he knew little of the soldier opposed to him, an officer trained in the French and Spanish wars, the defender of Arras against a Marshal of France, and an O'Neill of Ulster, full of vindictive loathing against the covenanting leader who had shed the innocent blood of the clansmen of Tyrowen, at Newry and at Island Magee. The whole forenoon of that memorable day was spent in repeated attacks by Munroe's troops, which were always steadily repulsed. O'Neill kept his men well in hand, and especially restrained his impetuous commander of horse, MacNeney, who burned to launch his riders upon the squadrons of Scottish cavalry. "Wait for the sun," O'Neill said, "when the sun begins to sink towards the west, then will the Lord' have delivered those covenanting scoundrels into our hands." Still the assaults continued, with loss and exhaustion on the part of the enemy, until the prudent Irish chief, who observed the sun that day, like an astronomer, saw that its rays were beginning to dart into the faces of the Scots. Now, steady, rapid, advance all along the line! And *now*, MacNeney, the spur in your horse's side, and the bridle upon his mane! In a few moments down went horse and foot, and there was no covenanting army any more, only a howling rabble rout, flying for their lives. They had need, for O'Neill, when he did move, was "hot upon the spur," and Monroe and a party of officers betook themselves to ignomi-

nious flight. The General lost his hat and wig; but eastward
still he urged his horse, through the marshes of the Montiaghs,
by the southern shore of Lough Neagh, across the Bann
about the place where the ghosts were still shrieking; and,
before morning, the Protestant burghers of Lisburn were dis-
turbed by the gallop of horses ready to founder. They looked
out of window; it was only General Monroe and staff making
their entry; but the frightened shopkeepers almost thought
that they heard at the town's end the thundering hoofs of
Owen Roe's riders. Three thousand Scottish and English men
fell on that day of Benburb, and the Irish nation felt that they
had got a leader able to cope with the Lord-General Cromwell.

As this affair of Benburb is creditable to Irish soldiership,
therefore Froude never alludes to it. The miserable Historian
is always anxiously on the watch to find some pretext for
goading our people with a taunt; and it is really wonderful to
observe how low down, and how far out of his way, he will
go to contrive a cutting and stinging gibe. For example, by
way of enforcing his favourite theory, that Irishmen require
to be used with severity, and that the more you scourge them
the more they love you, he quotes, what he calls a Hibernian
proverb, in Latin, to the effect that if you soothe and flatter an
Irishman he will stab you, but if you kick him he will be your
affectionate servant. Froude knows perfectly well that this is
a French proverb, which the proud *seigneurs* applied to their
serfs, and that it had no reference to Ireland at all—" *Oignez
vilain; il vous poindra; poignez vilain; il vous oindra.*"

But our kind Historian, finding the proverb turned into a
Latin hexameter, and perceiving that *Hibernicus* fits the
measure, cannot resist the temptation. The Irish, according
to him, made a proverb on themselves, proclaiming their own
dastard servility. They say to all mankind in this proverb—
Do us the pleasure, good sirs, to kick us, that we may have
the gratification of kissing your honours' boots! True, this is
a small matter; so is the omission of all mention of Benburb;
so is the taunt about the Irish paring their forests; yet these
things show the vicious *animus* of the creature. If he cannot
be always bombarding the Irish with cannon, he, at least, can
occupy himself in pricking them with needles.

CHAPTER VII.

"CLAN OLIVER."

Now came in the deluge of Cromwellians, who were termed by
the Irish *Clan Oliver*, as the invaders of Elizabeth's day had
been called sometimes Clan London, or Clan Sacsanagh.　It is
not my purpose to follow Froude through all his details relating
to the Cromwellian settlement, because this is rendered un-
necessary by the admirable work of Mr Prendergast; and
Froude has himself fully admitted in one place the accuracy of
Prendergast's facts and authorities, at the same time that, in
many other passages, he makes statements of his own utterly
at variance with those facts and authorities.　What is material
to point out here is, that the Historian most warmly approves
of the *régime* established by Cromwell in Ireland, only lamenting
that "he died too soon."　Speaking of that General and his
indiscriminate slaughters of soldiers and civilians, of men,
women, and children at Drogheda and Wexford, he says,
pathetically, "Happier far would it have been for Ireland, if,
forty years later, there had been a second Cromwell before
Limerick!"　It had been better, he thinks, if Sarsfield
and his men, and all the peaceful traders, and all the
heroic women of Limerick city had had their throats cut,
instead of being admitted to a Treaty.　Perhaps he is right,
seeing that the Treaty was to be instantly violated.　This
Historian does not mind being charged with bloodthirstiness :
on the contrary, he is flattered by it : he loves to write of
blood, and to urge on other people the duty of shedding it :
the odour of gore is grateful to his nostrils, whereas he despises
"rose-water," which is Carlyle's phrase to designate any kind
of gentleness or mercy, or even ordinary good faith observed
towards Papists.　Cromwell, he says with delight, did not

assuredly come to Ireland "to make war with rose-water."
No, it was the genuine red liquid, venous and arterial. There
is no part of the Cromwellian system which seems to give him
such heartfelt pleasure as the treatment of the priests. Only
it was too mild, and was applied for too short a time; if the
great statesman had but lived, there would soon have been not
a single priest left to "work mischief,"—which is his way of
describing the saying of Mass.

The good Father Burke, who is so amiable towards Froude,
must be all the while aware of how it would have fared with
himself if he had lived in the time of Froude's hero. Doubtless
it is the duty of a Christian divine to love all men, even his
enemies; and it was in this sense that he said he loved Froude.
But he knows very well that in Froude's political economy, his
(Father Burke's) head is exactly of the same value as the head
of a bitch-wolf; namely, six pounds sterling of the money of
that day, equal, we may say, to eighteen pounds of to-day.
And it will not do to say that Froude estimates the goods at
that price only, in the case that Father Burke had lived in the
latter part of the eighteenth century; for he regrets, passion-
ately, the too-early relaxation of that system; wishes there
had been a Cromwell before Limerick; wishes that there were
a Cromwell for Ireland's sake *now*: for, while the wolves were
cleared off entirely, there are priests in Ireland still. Evidently
while the wolf-price was enough, the priest's head-money ought
to have been raised. My own estimate of the value of Father
Burke's head differs from Froude's, and is based upon another
sort of tariff; for I hold it to be worth at least five hundred
heads of the Froudes. Let nobody deceive himself, however,
by assuming that this Historian discusses these matters in a
historic spirit, as matters whose interest is long past and gone
with the changing current of events. By no means: he treats
them in the spirit of a party pamphleteer, and with an obvious
intention to act upon the present politics and passions of men.
Thus, instead of giving a word of praise to the devoted clergy
who persisted in hearing confessions and administering
Sacraments, under the imminent penalty of transportation and
of death, he never mentions those wonderful men without
ribald abuse and calumny. "Priests and dispossessed pro-
prietors," he says, "were hiding in disguise among the tribes,

making mischief when they were able." He never alludes to the
deadly risks those clergy ran in staying by their flocks. Close
as has been his inspection of documents, in public record offices,
he never found the bills duly furnished by and paid to god-
fearing troopers for their captives—" To five priests captured
in the county of Cavan and sent in"—" To two priests *with
their appurtenances* [namely, books and caps and stoles] sent in
by Lieutenant Wood," and so-forth, to great length : for which
see Prendergast and Curry—you need not look to the Historian
of " The English in Ireland." He cannot help, indeed, mentioning some of the severe measures used against the clergy ;
he only affirms that not *so many* were transported as those who
were arrested ; but nobody had said there were.

As to the people actually transported from Ireland to
Barbadoes or other colonies or plantations, he, in his last lecture,
questions Father Burke's estimate of the numbers so exiled
within a few years. He says :—

" Father Burke says that Cromwell meant to exterminate
the Irish. I distinguish again between the industrious Irish
and the idle, fighting Irish. He showed his intention towards
the peasantry a few days after his landing, for he hung two of
his own troopers for stealing a hen from an old woman.
Cromwell, says the Father, wound up the war by taking
80,000 men and shipping them to the sugar plantations of
Barbadoes. In six years, such was the cruelty, that not
twenty of them were left. Eighty thousand men, Father Burke!
and in six years not twenty left! I have read the Thurlow
Papers, where the account will be found of these shipments
to Barbadoes. I can find nothing about 80,000 men there.
When were they sent out, and how, and in what ships ?"

I think, however, that Father Burke's estimate is not far
from correct ; though, to be sure, 80,000 is a large round
number. But it is well known that the deportation both of
priests and of laymen, of young men and maidens, was on a
very large scale. In consequence of the great increase of
priests towards the close of the year 1665, a general arrest
by the justices of the peace was ordered ; it was the sporting
season for priests, and even wolves were left comparatively at
peace for a time. " On the 3rd of May," says Prendergast,
" the governors of the respective precincts were ordered to

send them with sufficient guards from garrison to garrison to
Carrickfergus, to be there put on board such ships as should
sail with the first opportunity for the Barbadoes." Poor old
Father Paul Cashin, a very ancient and frail man, being apprehended at Maryborough, and sent on to Philipstown on the
way to Carrickfergus, there fell desperately sick, and was in
danger of perishing in a dungeon from want and hardship.
After months, the Commissioners ordered him an allowance of
sixpence a day; and when he should be well enough to move,
this allowance was to be continued to him during his journey
to Carrickfergus "in order to his transportation to the Barbadoes." It would not be much sugar Father Paul would
make after being set down there and bidden to take up the
shovel and the hoe; but the authorities thought that under a
Barbadoes planter he would at least be kept from "mischief"
—that is from Mass and Confession. The difficulty suggested
by Froude in the paragraph above cited, how and in what
ships were these 80,000 sent to Barbadoes? is not so very
serious a difficulty. The operation extended over several
years, and shipping was not so very scarce then, either in
England or in Ireland. Besides, Doctor Sir William Petty and
other adventurers were piling up all the shipyards in the
kingdom with the best of Irish timber. Still there was some
shortcoming in the tonnage available for this service, and it
cost too much, so that, on the 27th of February, 1657, the
Government referred it to the Lord-Lieutenant to consider
where the priests, then crammed into the prisons of Dublin,
might be most safely disposed of. And so they were carried
across the island, placed in boats, and flung out upon the bare
islands of Arran, in the Atlantic, and Innisbofin, off the coast
of Connemara, there to consider themselves, upon an allowance
of sixpence per day. It was when private enterprise came in
aid of the Government that no want or shipping was experi-
enced. The merchants of Bristol contracted with the Commissioners, not for cargoes of priests, but for young men and
marriageable girls, who would be more useful, these merchants
thought, upon their West India plantations. Ostensibly these
were to be all persons having no visible means of support,
but practically, it was a slave-hunt. Says Prendergast:—

"Messrs Sellick and Leader, Mr Robert Yeomans, Mr

Joseph Lawrence, and others, all of Bristol, were active agents. As one instance out of many :—Captain John Vernon was employed by the Commissioners for Ireland into England, and contracted in their behalf with Mr David Sellick and Mr Leader, under his hand, bearing date the 14th of September, 1653, to supply them with two hundred and fifty women of the Irish nation above twelve years, and under the age of forty-five; also three hundred men above twelve years of age, and under fifty, to be found in the country within twenty miles of Cork, Youghal, and Kinsale, Waterford and Wexford, to transport them into New England. Messrs Sellick and Leader appointed their shipping to repair to Kinsale; but Roger Boyle, Lord Broghill (afterwards Earl of Orrery), whose name, like that of Sir C. Coote, seems ever the prelude of woe to the Irish, suggested that the required number of men and women might be had from among the wanderers and persons who had no means to get their livelihood in the county of Cork alone. Accordingly, on the 23rd of October, 1653, he was empowered to search for them and arrest them, and to deliver them to Messrs Sellick and Leader, who were to be at the charge of conducting them to the water side, and maintaining them from the time they received them; and no person, being once apprehended, was to be released, but by special order in writing under the hand of Lord Broghill."

Many such operations took place in various parts of the country; until this Bristol firm alone had shipped above 6400 young strong people within the desirable ages. Many a girl of gentle birth and delicate nurture must have been seized by those slave-dealers and hurried to the private prisons. Daniel Connery, a gentleman of Clare County, was sentenced to banishment for harbouring a priest in 1657. "This gentleman had a wife and twelve children; his wife fell sick, and died in poverty. Three of his daughters, most beautiful girls, were transported to the West Indies, to an island called the Barbadoes; and there, if they are alive, they are in miserable slavery." (*Morison's Threnodia:* cited by Prendergast). On the whole, taking priests and laymen together, men and women, girls and boys, and allowing some years for the operation, I think we may allow Father Burke's estimate to be a fair and probable one.

But the matter, and perhaps the only matter, which disquiets and perplexes the mind of the " Historian," is the fact, that in the midst of all these horrors, Catholic priests were not only ministering all over the country, but coming in from France and Spain and Rome; not only supplying the *vacuum* made by transportation and by death, but keeping up steadily the needful communication between the Irish Church and its head; and not only coming, but going (both times incurring the risk of capital punishment), and not in commodious steamships, which did not then exist, but in small fishing luggers or schooners; not as first-class passengers, but as men before the mast. Archbishops worked their passage. The whole of this strange phenomenon, which continued more than a century, belongs to an order of facts, which never entered into the Historian's theory of human nature. It is a factor in the account that he can find no place for; he gives it up. Yet Edmund Spenser, long before this day, as good a Protestant as Froude, and an undertaker too upon Irish confiscated estates, had at least somewhat of the poetic vision and poetic soul. There were moods of his undertaking mind in which he could look upon such strange beings as these priests with a species of awe, if not with full comprehension. He much marvels at the zeal of these men, " which is a greate wonder to see how they spare not to come out of Spain, from Rome and from Remes, by long toyle and daungerous travayling hither, where they know perill of death awayteth them, and no reward or richesse." Mr Froude, indeed, speaks of them as engaged in nothing else but keeping up treasonable alliances with countries at war with England, and recruiting for foreign armies. As for their expecting no reward or richesse for such laborious service, he would bid you tell that to Judæus Apella, or to the horse marines !

Reward and richesse ! I know the spots, within my own part of Ireland, where venerable Archbishops hid themselves, as it were, in a hole of the rock. In a remote part of Louth County, near the base of the Fews mountains, is a retired nook called Ballymascanlon. There dwelt for years, in a farm house which would attract no attention, the Primate of Ireland and successor of St Patrick, Bernard MacMahon, a prelate accomplished in all the learning of his time, and assiduous in

the government of his archdiocese; but he moved with
danger, if not with fear, and often encountered hardships in
travelling by day and by night. His next successor, but one,.
was Michael O'Reilly, and he dwelt in a cabin at Termon-
fechin, near Clogher Head, a very wild place, and greatly out
of the way, as it lay between the Great Northern Road and
the sea, and could only be found by those who searched for it.
Here he died. And if such were the toils, hardships, and.
dangers of the highest ecclesiastics, we may conjecture what.
kind of life awaited the simple priests who devoted themselves
to the mission; yet it was with full knowledge of all this,.
with full resolution to brave all this, that many hundreds of
educated Irishmen, fresh from the colleges of Belgium or of
Spain, came to the French sea-coast at Brest or St Malo, bent
on finding some way of crossing to where their work lay.
Imagine a priest ordained at Seville or Salamanca, a gentleman of high old name, a man of eloquence and genius, who
has sustained disputations in the college halls on questions of
literature or theology; imagine him on the quays of Brest,.
treating with the skipper of some vessel to let him work his
passage; he wears tarry breeches and a tarpaulin hat (for
disguise was generally needful); he flings himself on board,
takes his full part in all hard work, scarce feels the cold spray
and the fierce tempests; and he knows, too, that the end of it
all, for him, may be a row of sugar canes to hoe, under the
blazing sun of Barbadoes, overlooked by a broad-hatted agent.
of a Bristol planter; yet he goes eagerly to meet his fate, for
he carries in his hand a sacred deposit, bears in his heart a.
sacred message, and must deliver it or die. Imagine him
then springing ashore, and repairing to seek the bishop of the
diocese in some cave, or behind some hedge, but proceeding.
with caution by reason of the priest-catchers and their wolf-
dogs. But Froude would say, this is the *ideal* priest you
have been portraying. *No*; it is the real priest as he existed
and acted at that day, and as he would again in the like
emergency. And is there nothing admirable in all this? Is
there not something superhuman and sublime? Ah! we
Protestants are certainly most enlightened creatures. Mr.
Froude says we are the salt of the earth. We stand, each of
us, with triumphant conceit, upon the sacred and inalienable

right of private stupidity; but I should wish to see our excellent Protestantism produce some fruit like this.

And not only has this Crusader no word of admiration or
commendation for the more than chivalrous bravery of the
priests who dared and defied the toil and the peril, humiliation,
transportation, and death, for the sake of feeding those flocks
which the English were shearing—not only does he pass over
in silence, or make light of, or attempt to deny, the frightful
persecutions continually inflicted upon those clergy, or hanging
over their heads, but the great leading theme of his whole
book, the thing which he most earnestly repeats is *this*—the
priests were never persecuted enough, except only in Cromwell's time! Ah! " if Oliver Cromwell had but left a son like
himself," he pathetically exclaims, Ireland's lot at this day had
been happier; and it would be now as easy to find a wolf in
the island as a priest. He is very hard indeed to satisfy in
the matter of persecution; for, although the laws for making
Ireland too hot to hold a priest were constantly elaborated and
made more atrocious nearly every year for the next century
after Cromwell, still there was occasional *connivance;* and those
obnoxious pastors were often left unpunished, and even their
saying of Mass was often winked at, provided they committed
the offence in some very obscure place; this does not suit the
Historian at all. He wants their hearts' blood; and it was
such "mistaken leniency" on the part of the government that
made Papists so insolent that they continually rose in new insurrections, and even at one time (when James the Second
came to the throne) their presumption rose to such a pitch
that he tells us with disgust, "the Irish thought *Ireland was
theirs.*"

It is to be feared that the Historian, after all his researches,
fails to comprehend the exact purpose and extent of those
occasional connivances or tolerations; the purpose was to keep
up an efficient machinery for getting a hold of more and more
of the lands which were still remaining in the hands of Papists,
under secret trusts or illegal leases. The Protestant interest
could not afford to suppress the Mass, so long as any Catholic
possessed an acre of land or a good horse. If there had been
no priests, and no Catholic service could anywhere be cele-
brated, it was feared that nearly all the Catholics would con-

form; and then, where would our Protestant interest be? Our good Protestants could no more afford to do without the Mass than without the "massacre." So, successive Viceroys and Lords of Council changed their policy from time to time, either suspending the operation of the most ferocious of the penal laws, or enforcing them in all their horror, as political exigencies for the time-being might seem to require. Mr Froude, with his unbending Protestant honesty, must really have some indulgence for people who, after doing the work of the Lord so well, felt that they had not yet received their full reward; for certain Papist Hittites, Edomites, and Amalekites, could still be found, by means of earnest and prayerful diligence, who were fraudulently receiving the rents and profits of their own estates, and thus cheating honest colonists. For these Amalekites it was needful to keep up a kind of secret hole-and-corner Mass; and the army of informers who were kept in pay might be trusted to find out who attended those useful ministrations. Here is the true key to the Penal Laws and to their administration.

Yes: evil must come of it, as this honest being truly apprehends. In his last lecture, by way of reply to Father Burke, he cannot conceal his uneasiness. He says:—

"England is afraid, however, and deeply afraid. She is afraid of being ever driven to use again those measures of coercion against Ireland, which have been the shame of her history."

The shame of her history, inasmuch as they were not duly executed. But what is England afraid of now? Ireland is very quiet, and so free from disturbance, and every sort of crime, that many a single county in England exhibits more murders, poisonings, burglaries, and waylayings with intent to murder, in one year than the whole of Ireland can show. What, then, thinks the Historian, is the provocation which is likely to drive his countrymen to new penal laws against Ireland? Can it be the Home Rule agitation—an agitation which is not only perfectly legal and constitutional, but also entirely harmless and useless? No; certainly not this. As for the outcry some Irishmen are making, claiming that they ought to be governed according to "Irish Ideas,"—governed *by England*, neither can this disquiet their English masters much. Their English masters know how to deal with such matters as these, by seizing on such newspapers as offend them, and by trying the most noisy of the agitators before packed juries? What, then, precisely, does the Historian's ominous threat portend? What does he wish his countrymen to do to us more? It may be that the learned and eloquent gentleman, having lived a good deal in Ireland of late, has observed that many industrious Irish people, grandsons and descendants of those who were once so thoroughly stripped bare, have gradually worked themselves into possession again of broad estates, often in the very tribe-lands of their own clans. Those estates were taken from their ancestors and given to the "saints" without money and without price: the present owners have won some of them back in the sweat of brow and brain. Catholics, too, having been plundered of their own Cathedrals, Churches and Abbey-lands, are now found in possession of new and splendid churches, and of great and beneficent religious houses. Here is a matter which is evidently worthy of the serious consideration of us, the enlightened Protestants; for if the earth is not our's and the fulness thereof, we should like to know to whom it does belong? Would not a good, prudent system of penal laws jockey those idolatrous Papists out of all they own, even as before? And is it any wonder that Historian Froude begins really to *fear* that England may be forced to resort to the old system of coercion once more?

Is this the explanation of his ominous menace, or is it merely, (as one of his English critics has insisted) a general craving on his part, "to burn or boil somebody, if only he could make up his mind whom to boil or burn." On this last question I do not really think the Historian labours under any doubt or difficulty. I know whom he wishes to cook.

At any rate, it really seems that this Crusader, like many another great man, is in advance of his age, or else behind it. He is either above the general level of human conscience and morals, or else below it. Either way, whether he is behind or before, whether too high or too low, his shot has failed to strike right between wind and water: and his crusade is a failure.

In one other article, I shall wash my hands of our Historian; and having washed shall slightly perfume them.

CHAPTER VIII.

RELIGIOUS LIBERTY IN IRELAND.

THE only period—and it was a very short period—in which
Liberty of Conscience was recognized in Ireland by express
law, from the time of Henry VIII. until the reign of Queen
Victoria—the *only* bright moment of respite—was that in
which the Parliament of King James II. sat in Dublin. And
this was the only Parliament that ever represented the Irish
nation even unto this day. For the Parliament elected after
"Emancipation," upon the basis of wholesale disfranchisement,
certainly did not represent Ireland; and neither has any one of
the Parliaments from that time to the present moment. That
famous Assembly was composed indifferently of Catholics and
Protestants, but Catholics in the great majority. Some
exclusive Protestant boroughs, whose Corporate authorities did
not admit a Catholic to live within their bounds, did not,
indeed, send any members. There was no representative from
Derry, nor from Coleraine. But Bandon sent two gentlemen
of the MacCarthy clan; Dublin, City and County, and the
University were represented, the County by Simon Luttrell
and Patrick Sarsfield; the City by Sir Michael Creagh, Lord
Mayor, and by Terence Dermot, Alderman; the College by
Sir John Meade and Michael Coghlan; the Borough of
Belfast by Marcus Talbot and Daniel O'Neill; Newry by
Rowland White and Rowland Savage; Down County by two
of the MacGennises. On the whole, I find in the roll of that
famous Parliament—the only genuine Parliament Ireland ever
saw—a large and liberal admixture of gentlemen of English
race and of Irish families; a list which it does one good to
read; Fitzgeralds and O'Reillys, O'Briens and Nugents,
Aylmers, Eustaces, and Archbolds. The borough of Wicklow
was represented by an O'Byrne and an O'Toole—very proper

members for that constituency. Naas, in Meath, returned Charles White and Walter, Lord Dongan, a near relative of that Thomas Dongan (properly O'Donegan), who had been obliged, a year before, to resign his office as Governor of New York; and he was the best Governor New York ever had. There were but six or seven Protestants in the House of Commons; but in the House of Peers we find besides the temporal Lords four Protestant Bishops, Meath, Ossory, Limerick, and Cork. Mr Froude counts amongst them the Bishop "of Munster;". (I quote Scribner's edition); but there never was any Bishop of Munster; and the Historian must mean Dr Dopping, Bishop of Meath, who is his especial favourite amongst all the Irish episcopacy, being in fact the very Bishop who shortly afterwards, on the conclusion of the Treaty of Peace, preached before the Court in Christ Church Cathedral, on the sinfulness of observing any compacts or treaties with Papists. The greater number of the Protestant Peers absented themselves, as they were generally devoted adherents to the usurper, the Prince of Orange. Substantially, however, there was a good and respectable representation of the Irish nation at that day.

This is a matter perplexing and even disgusting to the Impostor Historian; so he passes it over very lightly. Yet the acts of that assembly deserve to be held in remembrance a little. One of its earliest enactments was " an Act for securing Liberty of Conscience, and repealing such acts or clauses in any Act of Parliament which are inconsistent with the same." I need not here dwell upon the other measures passed by that excellent Parliament—an Act declaring the Parliament of England incapable of binding Ireland; an Act repealing the unjust Navigation Laws; an Act for attainder of rebels—that is, of persons who had borne arms against their Sovereign King James; an Act for removing all incapacities and disabilities of the natives of this kingdom, &c. For the present, it is enough to attend to the Act for Liberty of Conscience, and to see how the English Historian deals with that:—

" We hereby decree that it is the law of this land of Ireland that neither now, nor ever again, shall any man be prosecuted for his religion."

This looks plain enough; sounds fair and straightforward;

but the British Historian has found out the secret and malign intention : he says in his book—and it is the only notice he takes of the Act for Liberty of Conscience :—

" In harmony with the *language* which James had ingeniously used to advance Romanism behind principles which were abjured in every Catholic country of Europe, laws interfering with liberty of conscience were declared repealed."

What an artful tyrant! Not only to invent such *ingenious language*, declaring that no man should be punished for his religion, but also to impress this cunning artifice of speech upon his Parliament in Ireland! There may be some persons who could wish that Oliver Cromwell could have learned this sort of ingenious language, instead of saying to General Taaffe, who attempted to stipulate for liberty of conscience before surrendering Ross :—" I meddle," said Cromwell, " with no man's conscience ; but if, by liberty of conscience, you mean liberty to exercise the Mass, I judge it best to use plain dealing, and let you know that where the Parliament of England has power, *that* will not be allowed."

And, what a blessing it would have been if the grandfather of this same James the Second had learned, in his day, the use of that " language " (for there was nothing in it, Mr Froude assures us, but empty words), instead of issuing his famous proclamation of the 4th of July, 1605, wherein he " declared to his beloved subjects of Ireland that he would not admit any such liberty of conscience as they were made to expect."

Froude's account of the matter is that King James had committed to memory certain vile, hypocritical phrases about freedom of conscience—probably under the tuition of sóme Jesuit—in order " to advance Romanism *behind* those principles." What advancing of Romanism did he ever seek, either in England or in Ireland? He did wish to be at liberty to go to church himself, *behind those principles ;* he wished such of his subjects as chose to be Catholics to be free to hear Mass, and make Confession without being fined, whipped, pilloried, or transported! But neither he nor any Government official in his reign, whether in England or in Ireland, *ever* sought to injure, punish, or disfranchise any Protestant for *not* going to Mass.

F

In fact, the thing which offends our English Historian the most, and admonishes him to touch lightly on that whole subject, and drop it like a hot potato, is the fact that King James's own actions, and the measures of the Parliament which he called, and the administration of law in the High Courts of the Kingdom, were all guided and governed by the very same ingenious "language." Here was the infernal cunning of it. That Jesuit who tutored the King, I daresay, thought himself a deep schemer ; but no Romish devices can escape the searching probe of Froude.   In his last New York lecture he says of King James :—

" He was meditating the restoration of Popery in England, and he *took up* with toleration that he might introduce Catholics, under cover of it, into high offices of state, and bribe the Protestant Nonconformists to support him."

And so he advanced the treacherous declaration for liberty of conscience only to advance Romanism behind that principle ! And what did James the First, what did Oliver Cromwell, then wish to advance behind those opposite principles of *No liberty of conscience?*   It must have been Protestantism they wanted to advance ; or, at any rate, the Protestant interest.   But, after all, what was this insidious form of words which the Jesuits had invented for King James ?   Mr Froude does not give it ; but here it is :—

"KING JAMES'S SPEECH TO BOTH HOUSES OF PARLIAMENT IN IRELAND, PUBLISHED BY HIS MAJESTY'S ORDER, MAY 10TH, 1689.

" My Lords and Gentlemen,—The exemplary loyalty, which this nation express to me, at a time when others of my subjects so undutifully behaved themselves to me, or so basely betrayed me ; and your seconding my deputy as you did, in his bold and resolute asserting my right, and preserving this kingdom for me, and putting it in a posture of defence, made me resolve to come to you, and to venture my life with you, in the defence of your liberty and my right ; and to my great satisfaction I have not only found you ready and willing to serve me, but that your courage has equalled your zeal.   *I have always been for liberty of conscience,* and against invading any man's property ; having still in my mind the saying of holy writ, ' Do as you

would be done by; for that is the law and the prophets.' It
was this liberty of conscience I gave which my enemies both
at home and abroad dreaded, especially when they saw that I
was resolved to have it established by law in all my dominions,
and made them set themselves up against me, though for dif-
ferent reasons, seeing that if I had once settled it, my people,
in the opinion of the one, would have been too happy, and in
the opinion of the other, too great. This argument was made
use of to persuade their own people to join with them, and too
many of my own subjects to use me as they have done; but
nothing shall ever persuade me to change my mind as to that;
and wheresoever I am master, I design, God willing, to establish it by law, and to have no other test or distinction but that
of loyalty. I expect your concurrence in so Christian a
work, and in making effectual laws against profanings
and debauchery. I shall also most readily consent to the
making such good and wholesome laws as may be for
the general good of the nation, the improvement of trade,
and the relieving such as have been injured by the late
acts of settlement, as far forth as may be consistent with
reason, justice, and the public good of my people. And
as I shall do my part to make you happy and rich, so I make
no doubt of your assistance, by enabling me to oppose the unjust designs of my enemies, and to make this nation flourish.
And to encourage you the more to it, you know with how
great generosity and kindness the most Christian king gave a
secure retreat to the queen, my son, and self, when we were
forced out of England, and came to seek protection and safety
in his dominions; how he embraced my interest, and gave
supplies of all sorts, as enabled me to come to you, which,
without his obliging assistance, I could not have done; this he
did at a time when he had so many and so considerable
enemies to deal with; and so still continues to do. I shall
conclude as I began, and assure you, I am as sensible as you
can desire me of the signal loyalty you have exprest to me,
and shall make it my chief study, as it always has been, to
make you and all my subjects happy."

Here the designing creature actually says that he had been,
at all times, for liberty of conscience; and the puzzling matter
to the Froudes is that he had been so in fact; of which one

illustration was seen, even here on Manhattan Island—such was the malign cunning of that artful tyrant, in spreading far and wide over the dependencies of the British crown, that same shocking delusion of liberty of conscience.

When King James was Duke of York, in the reign of his brother Charles, he was "Proprietary Governor" of the Province of New York, and in the year 1682 he commissioned Colonel Thomas Dongan, of an ancient Irish family, who had commanded a regiment in the French service, to proceed to New York as his Lieutenant or Resident Governor. He proceeded at once, according to his instructions, to issue his warrants for the election of a General Assembly. This was an auspicious beginning of his administration, as it was a concession from the Duke of New York for which the people had long struggled. This illustrious body, consisting of the Governor, ten Councillors, and seventeen Representatives elected by the people, assembled in the city of New York on the 17th of October, 1683. As he was the first, so he was the most liberal and friendly royal Governor that presided over the popular legislatures of New York; and the contests between arbitrary power and popular rights, which distinguished the administration of future Governors, down to the Revolution, did not have their origin under his administration. The first act of this General Assembly was the framing of a charter of liberties—the first guarantee of popular government in the province. This noble charter ordained:

"That supreme legislative power should for ever reside in the Governor, Council, and people, met in General Assembly; that every freeholder and freeman might vote for Representatives without restraint; that no freeman should suffer but by the judgment of his peers, and that all trials should be by a jury of twelve men; that no tax should be assessed, on any pretext whatever, but by the consent of the Assembly, that no seaman or soldier should be quartered on the inhabitants against their will; that no martial law should exist; that no person, professing faith in God, by Jesus Christ, should, at any time, be in any way *disquieted or questioned for any difference of opinion in matters of religion.*"

So Colonel Dongan also had learned the ingenious language which King James had been taught by that "Jesuit!"

There had been penal laws in force against Catholics in all these provinces; and seeing that Governor Dongan was himself a Catholic, and desired the liberty of going to church without penal consequences, just as James himself always wished, he thought it would be no harm if the people of New York could be prevailed upon to let one another alone on that one matter, at least. He had a great amount of popular prejudice and ignorance to encounter; and there was plenty of jealousy and ill-will against him as a "Papist;" yet as he was, in fact, not only a very good and honourable gentleman, but also a most zealous and efficient Governor, as all authorities agree, he did succeed in procuring the adoption of that famous charter. The clause assuring religious liberty was found to hurt nobody, and people lived peaceably enough under it, until what is called the abdication of King James, in England, and the invasion by William of Orange. Then the Governor retired from office. He perceived that the days of "Ascendancy" and the Protestant interest were returning, and he went to live quietly on Staten Island, where he had a cottage and a mill. But he was not to be allowed to escape observation in this retreat; a revolutionary government, called a "Committee of Safety," was established in the city; Catholics were hunted down in every direction, and orders were issued for the arrest of Governor Dongan. He took refuge on board a vessel in the harbour, where he remained in concealment many weeks. In the meantime his servants were arrested and his effects seized at his residence. The "Charter of Liberties," passed in 1683, under a Catholic governor, was repealed, with all other laws passed by the late General Assembly of New York in 1691, and a so-called "Bill of Rights" passed, which expressly deprived Catholics of all their political and religious *rights*. In 1697 this "Bill of Rights" was repealed, "probably as being too liberal," says Bishop Bayley; and in 1700, an Act was passed which recited that "Whereas, divers Jesuits, priests, and Popish missionaries have of late come, and for some time have had their residence in the remote parts of this province, and others of his Majesty's adjacent colonies, who, by their wicked and subtle insinuations, industriously laboured to debauch, seduce, and withdraw the Indians from their due obedience to his most sacred Majesty, and to excite and stir them up to sedition, rebellion, and open hostility against his Majesty's Government;" and enacted that every priest, etc., remaining in or coming into the province after November 1st, 1700, should be "deemed and accounted an incendiary and disturber of the public peace and safety, and an enemy of the true Christian religion, and shall be adjudged to suffer *perpetual imprisonment;*" that, in case of escape and capture, they should suffer *death;* and that harbourers of priests should pay a fine of two hundred pounds, and stand three days in the pillory.

In short, the Penal Laws of England and Ireland were carefully copied by the Colonists on this side the Atlantic. Even in Maryland, whose Catholic founders had made liberty of conscience an organic law, the same scenes of persecution were now enacted; and it need not be said that New England was ready to go all lengths against Papists, and against Protestants, too, if they were not the right kind of Protestants.

It may not be so generally known as it ought to be how zealously and steadily our worthy Protestant Colonists followed the examples set them across the ocean, for the greater part of a century. Many persons vainly suppose that the series of Penal Laws in Ireland, with which we are all so familiar, were invented for the sole sake of our countrymen. Let such persons read the following from the Statute Books of Virginia :—

"1753.—An Act for reducing the several laws made for establishing the General Court, and for regulating and setting the proceedings therein into one Act of Assembly.

"*Recusant, Convict, Disabled to be a Witness.*

"XXIV. That Popish recusant, convicts (that is, convicted of recusancy), shall be incapable to be witnesses in any cause whatsoever.

"1756.—An Act for disarming Papists and reputed Papists refusing to take the oaths to the Government.

"*No Papist to keep Arms, etc.*

"III. And for the better securing the lives and properties of his Majesty's faithful subjects, be it further enacted and declared, That no Papist or reputed Papist, so refusing or making default as aforesaid, shall or may have or keep in house or elsewhere, or in the possession of any other person to his use, or at his disposition, any arms, weapons, gunpowder, or ammunition, other than such necessary weapons as shall be allowed to him, by order of the Justices of the Peace, at their court, for the defence of his house or person.

" No Papist to keep any Horse above the Value of £5.

" VIII. And be it further enacted, That no Papist, or reputed Papist, so refusing or making default as aforesaid, at any time after the first day of July, in the year of our Lord one thousand seven hundred and fifty-six, shall or may have or keep in his own possession, or in the possession of any other person to his use or at his disposition, any horse or horses which shall be above the value of five pounds, to be sold; and that any two or more Justices of the Peace, from time to time, by warrant under their hands and seals, may and shall authorize any person or persons, with the assistance of the constable where the search shall be (who is hereby required to be aiding and assisting herein), to search for and seize for his Majesty and his successors, all such horses, which horses are hereby declared to be forfeited to his Majesty and his successors. The Acts of Assembly now in force in the Colony of Virginia, Williamsburg, 1760.

"Negroes, mulattoes, and Indians not to be sworn as witnesses against whites."

But Catholics could not be witnesses, even against negroes.

But all this is a mere digression, scarcely worth dwelling upon in this place, but that we happen to be here, in the State of New York, which is now happily under the *regime* imagined by the Catholic Governor Dongan; and also that the story of this estimable Governor, coinciding, as it does, with the efforts made for freedom by King James at home, may help to illustrate a truth which is an ugly one to have to admit, namely, that religious persecution is the very essence of Protestantism. Perhaps this is natural, and all right; for we, being the enlightened portion of Christendom, must feel ourselves authorized, and indeed *called*, to make ourselves think our thoughts, and go our way, or else " to burn them and to boil them."

It is time to drop this offensive and irritating subject. Nothing would be easier than to demonstrate the excessive bad faith and malign intention which the " Historian " has brought to the narration of the reign of King James the Second, and the measures of his excellent Parliament. Of course the principal witness to all the cruelties alleged to have been inflicted upon "the Protestants," in that reign, is Archbishop King (*State of the Protestants of Ireland*).   According to his usual system, Mr Froude palms off upon his leaders a bad and discredited authority, suppressing all others.   It need not be said that the author who cited Sir John Temple, without telling how that wretch afterwards attempted to suppress his own book, should a little further on give us the frightful fables of King without telling us that the man had composed his book, after King James's fall, to help the confiscations, to stimulate the penal laws, and to win his mitre; and without mentioning that a worthy clergyman of King's own church, who dwelt in Ireland and had full knowledge of passing events, was seized with a sacred wrath on reading that bad book of the Archbishop, and demonstrated (to use his own words) that it contained " scarcely a true word." Such is precisely the species of authority that Froude chooses to rely upon; and, therefore, when his next and last volume comes forth, his readers may expect that he will dose them with plenty of Sir Richard Musgrave.

Perhaps I should never have undertaken to expose any of the delinquencies of Froude, but that the excellent Father Burke, in his most admirable course of lectures, dealt so gently with the impostor, and even admitted his honesty and good faith. Father Burke's lectures, as I read them now in their collected form, appear to me a most complete answer, and most scathing rebuke; a work, indeed, which will live while the Irish race lives.   If I have ventured to come forward into the same field, it has been mainly with a view of exhibiting not the honesty and good faith, but the determined dishonesty and treachery of that pretended "Historian;" and to show that all this has been perpetrated with the odious intention of affronting and scandalizing a whole race and nation. I am not so good a Christian as Father Burke; and it gives me pleasure to think that I may have contributed a little to destroy such remnant of credit as Froude had, whether at home or abroad.

He has done evil as he could; he has sought grievously to injure a people which has done him no wrong; and I would now counsel him—after the example of his Cromwellian heroes—to fall down upon his knees, and "seek the Lord," and wrestle nightly with the Lord, so that, peradventure, grace might be given him to repent, and confess, and receive absolution of his sin.

DUNN AND WRIGHT, PRINTERS, GLASGOW.

Milton Keynes UK
Ingram Content Group UK Ltd.
UKHW020114030823
426179UK00005B/153